MAJOR LEAGUE *Shutout Debut*

A Look Back After 60 Years

A MEMOIR

DON LOUN

WATTWIL PRESS

DISCLAIMER: The information contained in this book is for informational purposes only. It is not intended to substitute for professional, knowledgeable coaching and teaching. Individual physical, mental and medical situations must be assessed and evaluated before trying any strategies mentioned. The author disclaims any, and all, liability arising directly or indirectly from the use of any information included in this book. Any instructional strategies, workout tips, and exercises worked for the author, and may not be suitable for every individual.

Copyright © 2024 by Don Loun

All rights are reserved. Neither this book, nor any portion thereof, may be reproduced, or used in any manner whatsoever, without the express, written permission of the author, except for the use of brief quotations in critical articles and reviews.

ISBN: 979-8-218-38765-5

Printed in the USA.

Cover and Interior Design by Tami Boyce (tamiboyce.com)

For my family

TABLE OF CONTENTS

Introduction · ix

Part One
Growing Up on Both Sides of the Tracks in Frederick, Maryland · · · · · · 1

1 Mush · 3
2 Mom · 9
3 Liquor Store Rumble · 13
4 Pop Pop · 17
5 Brother Bob · 25
6 Potato Chip League · 27
7 Three-Fingered Glove · 31
8 Ike · 33
9 Mount Carmel Little League · 35
10 Daydreaming · 39
11 Challenges · 41
12 Bing · 45
13 Optimist Club · 47
14 Tryouts · 51
15 An Untimely Setback · 55
16 Two-Wheeled Convertible · 57
17 Wake Up Call · 61
18 Close Encounters · 63
19 Wild as a Killdeer · 67
20 Foul Ball · 71
21 A Flickering Star · 75
22 Stay on the Mound · 81

Part Two
My Professional Baseball Career Washington Senators Organization — 1961 to 1969 · 87

23 Making the Cut · 89
24 Getting Paid to Play · 93

25	Hopkins Boarding House	97
26	First Start, First Shutout	99
27	Temptations	103
28	Lake Wales Rumble	105
29	Thanks, Joe	107
30	Paul Raybon	109
31	Liar Liar	111
32	Selma 1962	117
33	Ozark	121
34	Fred Waters	123
35	You Don't Decide Your Future	125
36	Duty Calls	129
37	Best Record	131
38	Turning Point	135
39	Unwritten Rule	141
40	First Triple A Spring Training	145
41	Why Not the Big Leagues?	147
42	The Fine	149
43	National Baseball Hall of Fame	151
44	The Chief	155
45	Who Is Asleep at the Wheel?	157
46	Welcome to the Show	159
47	Major League Shutout	163
48	New Gear	169
49	Big League Banter	171
50	You Had to Be There to See It	175
51	Dodger Invasion	179
52	Diamonds in the Rough	183
53	A Trapped Mouse	185
54	Montezuma's Revenge	189
55	Aloha!	193
56	Royal Treatment	199
57	Great Balls of Fire	201
58	I Can't Help Myself	203
59	Lowlights of Hawaii	207
60	Good Times	209

61	Wiener Truck	211
62	Fred Valentine	215
63	New Wind Up	217
64	Sacrificial Lamb	221
65	Close Shave	227
66	Chaos?	231
67	Game Over	233

Part Three
Opinions and Insights on the Game · · · · · · · 237

68	Changes	239
69	Scouts	243
70	Options	247
71	Pitching Staff	251
72	The Sponge	257
73	Umpires	259
74	Appreciation	263

Part Four
Pitching Specifics and More · · · · · · · 265

75	Thinking about Pitching?	267
76	Hold On	269
77	Hide It	273
78	Delivery	275
79	Mound Up	279
80	Control Yourself	281
81	Strike Zone	283
82	Advanced and Game Situations	285
83	Advanced—Pick Off Moves and More	289
84	Final Thoughts	291
85	Don Loun Pitching Stats (1961-69)	293

Epilogue · · · · · · · 295
Mostly Familiar Names · · · · · · · 301
Acknowledgments · · · · · · · 305

INTRODUCTION

I am not a writer. Storyteller, I think so. I have a decent memory of a period in my life that I revisit in my dreams regularly. I had the opportunity to play professional baseball and pursued it with total commitment and dedication.

For years, I wanted a sports writer to write my story as I experienced it. Most of them recommended I tell my own story. If you are not a writer, it's pretty tough to write your own story. I have notebooks filled with handwritten notes that I started 10 years ago. For years I kept refining the first part and never got past first base. Later, two-fingered typing helped me progress slightly but I had many more memories. When I began to dictate my stories I could finally express myself comfortably. If it seems like I am talking to you, I am.

This memoir traces my baseball career in the 1960s when I signed a professional contract with Washington's expansion Senators and played baseball with the organization for almost 9 years.

After pitching a shutout against the Boston Red Sox in my Major League debut, what happened? That is the million dollar question that friends, colleagues and others ask me. I was on a clear path to the Majors and had every weapon in my arsenal of pitches. Why was my success so short-lived?

Major League Shutout Debut

My story begins with my childhood because I think the child I was, and the adult I became, is totally reflected in my upbringing and the opportunities my hometown, Frederick, Maryland, offered. I believe that my story mirrors the lives of many hopeful guys like me who tried to make it happen when they had their shot.

My baseball years are filled with memories of life on and off the field. Sixty years later, some details are as clear as if they happened yesterday and others are getting a little foggy. I am thankful I started collecting my stories over ten years ago.

My recollections and opinions are not intended to insult, injure or embarrass anyone. I did not have an inside track on how decisions were made so my story is always from my point of view. It is not a glossy picture of an era of baseball nor the story of a baseball legend. But, I am in the Hall of Fame, sort of.

There are painful lessons that I learned along the way, and lessons that future players should pay attention to, and learn, from my story. In fact, writing this memoir has exposed some of my own misunderstandings and misperceptions. It should be pretty obvious while reading when I have an occasional rant.

My story is for my family, so that they know me and understand me better. The way we live today is so different from the way I grew up. I wanted to draw a clearer picture for them.

My story is also for my hometown of Frederick, Maryland. I never would have developed into the athlete that I was without the helping hands and opportunities that came my way.

My story is for all the players who have big dreams. Keep dreaming and working toward your goals. Keep your eyes wide open. Pay attention to what people are asking you to do because they may not be in your best interest. Be aware. Ask questions. Look out for yourself and make healthy choices.

Introduction

My story ends with pitching specifics for players, coaches, parents and students of the game. It is a compilation of what I learned over nine years of playing professional baseball as a left-handed pitcher. Play ball!

Part One

GROWING UP ON BOTH SIDES OF THE TRACKS IN FREDERICK, MARYLAND

1

MUSH

What was your earliest childhood memory? Mine was visiting Smoky, a live black bear, who lived in a cage outside of Delphey's Sport Store by Carroll Creek near the Barbara Fritchie house. I was with Mom, Aunt Nan and cousin Betty Jane on a warm, summer day. At three years old, it was amazing to see a live black bear. If wildlife in the area was injured, Delphey's arranged rehabilitation at a nearby sanctuary, I was told. I wonder what happened to Smoky.

Betty Jane climbed in the birdbath outside of Delphey's and kept the birds from drinking the water. When Mom wanted to take our picture, I frowned and refused because Betty Jane would not get out. Years later, guess what? I found a photograph of us together by the birdbath!

Even though I have looked at numerous historical photographs of my hometown, I have never seen a photograph of Smoky, the bear that I so vividly "remember."

Major League Shutout Debut

Betty Jane and me

Until I started school, I was shuffled between the country and the city. My mother worked three jobs as a single parent. We lived in a rented apartment near All Saints Street and South Market Street, which was known, at the time, as "the section." My Uncle Joe and his wife, Aunt Eva, lived across the hall from us in another apartment, but we shared a bathroom. Because of my mother's long working hours, she sent me to live in the country with Uncle Joe's mother-in-law, Grandma Shipe. It was too difficult to have two children, three jobs, and no transportation. I was young and well behaved, and my brother was three years older, and in school already.

Mush

Grandma met me at our third-floor apartment where Aunt Eva cared for me when my mother went to work early. Grandma and I always walked across the street to the train station for our short trip to Brunswick, where she lived. I don't recall much about the train except that there was lots of black smoke, it smelled bad, and it was noisy. The train station in Brunswick was just as bad.

Grandma lived in a weathered two-story house that badly needed repairs. I was treated well even though it was tough being separated from my mother and brother. Grandma took good care of me and my life was calm. Grandma baked bread every morning. She made rolls that looked like little chef hats. She taught me how to make a cereal called "mush" that I have not been able to find a recipe for, but she made it, especially for me. My job was to stir the mush so it did not burn or stick to the pan. She introduced me to snow cream which we could only eat after the first snow. I stayed warm and healthy during the early years of separation.

My mother visited about every two weeks when I was with Grandma. It was expensive to get a ride to Brunswick and Mom did not have a car. The options were: car, if you could get a ride; Trailways or Greyhound bus; or train. When the weather was bad, it didn't take much to be snowed in. It was dangerous on the poorly maintained country roads, and, if you had bad tires and no chains, you really couldn't travel. Uncle Joe drove my mother to Brunswick when he could. When she arrived, we would cry, and it was always gut wrenching to say goodbye.

My mother had a friend who wanted to adopt me in the event that my mother could not support all of us. Mom declined the offer but both of them visited me in Brunswick anyway. Mom's friend was very well-endowed. When they arrived, I was always excited to see her, too. I laugh now, but it was a comfort to me at that age to have many people care about me.

Major League Shutout Debut

We had a trunk farm by the railroad tracks in Brunswick. It was near the great Potomac River. A trunk farm is rich soil that is washed up when the river rises. We used to farm it even though it was not officially ours. When there were heavy rains, the farmers would give up their topsoil voluntarily as they had no control over the erosion. We planted vegetables in the rich soil. The most difficult part of working in the trunk garden was the unbearable mosquitoes that ate us alive. We tolerated it for a while and then hurried back to the house. I learned where good topsoil was located if it was needed for a small garden. I carried the soil in a partially filled water bucket, which was heavy, but I could handle it by myself.

Grandma had a big dog, and I loved to feed him. I visualized that I might be able to ride that dog because he was so sturdy. When I actually tried to ride him, he was very gentle and did not object. We grew up as pals, Horse and Rider. I imagined myself to be a cowboy in every sense of the word. I loved listening to the "Sons of Pioneers" on the radio. Horse and I played "gun and holster." I was thrilled to get a straw hat during the summer— every cowboy had a hat! I never had boots because we couldn't afford them but I did have fancy gloves with fringe on them. Grandma cut holes in fabric and added rubber bands to make a mask like the Lone Ranger's mask. My love for the cowboys was a part of my life then, and still is today.

Behind Grandma's house was a brickyard. The truckers loaded bricks using tongs to lift heavy stacks of bricks onto the truck. The men let me help by lifting one brick at a time with the heavy tongs. The men let me do that as long as I stayed out of the way so they could finish loading the truck. Sometimes I would earn a nickel but eventually I would have to get out of the way because I was so little.

Brick. Who knew that this would be my first introduction to brick? Later in my life, I would have a 36 year career in the brick industry in sales and management. I worked for many of the largest brick manufacturing companies in the world, including General Shale Brick, the largest company. Interestingly, the same man who gave me a start in the brick industry as an adult was also a mentor who encouraged me to play baseball. Harry Baker.

2

MOM

My father's birthday was November 9. Same as mine. On the day I was born he deserted my mother and left her with a three-year-old son and a newborn, me. He claimed I was not his child.

Since I was a November baby, Mom did not want me to start school at five years and ten months. However, it was stressful to keep me away from her in Brunswick. I was legally eligible to start school, so I did, and our small family stayed together.

During the Brunswick years, Mom had been a waitress at a popular quick stop sandwich shop called Pop Pooles Restaurant. She also stocked merchandise and did inventory at two five and dime stores, SS Kresge and McCrory's. Her jobs were convenient to the apartment and she could walk there in about five minutes. If she got extra hours, she was lucky because our relatives next door would watch my brother, and me, when I came to town.

Major League Shutout Debut

When the A & P grocery store came to Frederick, Mom started working there part time as a checker. Because she was available to be on call, she got full-time work rather quickly. She had additional training in Chambersburg Pennsylvania to become a meat wrapper. She later became a meat cutter, usually a man's job in those days. She worked there for almost 20 years and earned a well-deserved pension when she retired.

When I was about 10 years old, Mom and I were at the Frederick fairgrounds, and she spotted my father. She asked me if I wanted to see him and pointed to where he was standing. I had a brief glimpse, but wasn't interested in meeting him.

Mom's life was a struggle with so many jobs. She was fortunate to have friends and relatives who helped out as much as they could, considering they had problems of their own.

In 1945 my mother met my future stepfather, and they tied the knot. Our lives began to knit together. I called Robert L. Hoffman "Dad." He was a loyal family man and proud of my accomplishments. He was employed at Sears and later moved onto Fairchild Aircraft Company in Hagerstown. Being together for dinner was a special time to catch up. Trips to the beach meant Mom and Dad would get up in the middle of the night to prepare. Mom fried chicken while Dad packed the car. We always left before sunrise to avoid the traffic to the eastern shore. Holidays were special times I remember. My favorite Christmas was the year I got my bicycle. I had wanted one for a long time, but never thought we could afford it. I was absolutely thrilled. Mom only let me ride it in the country though, never in town.

When Mom worked Friday nights, we stayed at Aunt Catherine's house, Dad's sister. On Saturdays we enjoyed the activities around The Optimist Boys Club. Aunt Catherine introduced my brother and I to chocolate waffles which she made for

Mom

us when we stayed over. Sometimes she was called unexpectedly to the hospital where she worked as a nurse. No waffles that day!

When I was well into my baseball career, I met my father for the first time. He recognized the strong physical resemblance between us, and agreed that I was surely his son. A reserved friendship developed after that meeting.

Mom instilled in my brother and myself values of how to treat people and how to behave. Because we lived in a dangerous neighborhood, she taught us to be careful and stay away from trouble. She always did the best she could.

3

LIQUOR STORE RUMBLE

Our apartment in the city was in a dangerous part of town referred to as "the section." It was across the street from the train station, located on the third floor, high above a liquor store. I was warned to stay off our high porch because it was rickety and slippery. A scary, but memorable incident occurred when I was somewhere between four and five years old.

On Friday nights, groups of men would gather in the small "courtyard" to drink whiskey and shoot craps. There were rusty nail kegs scattered around for seating with empty whiskey bottles littering the dirt floor. Usually, I stayed inside the apartment while mom worked, but on this particular Friday night, I heard voices, loud voices, louder voices, so close I couldn't resist going out on the high porch. As instructed, if I ever went on a high porch, I was told to never go near the fragile banisters that connected the porch and the adjoining apartments. Aunt Eva and Uncle Joe were next door, so for a while, I was alone, and so curious.

Cautiously, I squeezed through the door onto the porch and backed up to the icebox. The conversations below me grew angry. I heard harsh language I didn't recognize, but I knew that some people were very unhappy. Crashing sounds were everywhere. Someone was upset with the outcome of the game, I imagined. Therefore, corrective measures needed to be taken. I cleverly had it figured out and I was only four years old. Trouble in the yard was common. But tonight, I was on the high porch and so curious.

As I backed up against the icebox, I remained fearful to venture near the banister. I was always a kid who didn't defy my elders, nor the people I respected: Santa Claus, Easter Bunny, cop on the corner, motorcycle policeman, pastor at the church, and my Sunday School teacher. I was sitting there quietly, while voices were getting louder.

Suddenly, a grunt, a groan, a moan. I heard loud whispers, shuffling feet and squeaky kegs across the concrete. Something bad had happened. There was a flurry of excitement with crying, yelling, and running. The liquor store door slammed over and over again.

It was quiet in the courtyard. I thought I heard soft, moaning, and groaning. I was frightened, afraid to be seen. Suddenly in the distance were red, yellow and green flashing lights. Ambulance sirens were blasting. The screams in the courtyard paralyzed.

I could only imagine what was going on as I sat there shivering, dazed and bewildered. I pictured the police and doctors carrying a bloodied, dead man on a stretcher. I imagined the victim rising up over three flights of stairs, in the air, covered with flour, as white as a bedsheet, flapping wings to usher him to heaven. I thought almost everyone went to heaven, but maybe they didn't get in the pearly gates. That image probably came from the Evangelical Church we attended at the time.

It was not long before calm returned to the courtyard. It seemed like everyone had left the area. It was so quiet I could hear crickets chirping. The evening rumble was over. Fear of the high porch continued, but I avoided it in the future. No more spying on the Friday night crapshoot for this little guy.

4

POP POP

When I was about seven years old my grandfather, Arthur "Doc" Ray, bought a house and small farm in the country. It was around 15 acres of good farmland about 4 1/2 miles east of town.

My grandfather, whom we fondly called "Pop Pop," and my Uncle Elmer, cleared the land. The farm was in rough shape and too much for Pop Pop to do alone. He never weighed over 119 pounds his entire life. The only two sports I remember him playing were horseshoes and duckpin bowling. Horseshoes would have been natural because he was, first and foremost, a blacksmith!

Pop Pop, known as "Doc" by everyone else, refurbished the old blacksmith shop on the farm and named it Hawk's Blacksmith Shop as it had previously been called. He fashioned iron tools, wagon wheel axles, everything you needed to build a wagon; the kind you would need for your horses.

The old home place

Quite a bit of his business involved bartering, but that was not sustainable long-term. Later, he worked at the Frederick Iron and Steel Company making iron tools. He moved on to Key Chevrolet Car Dealership where he built and repaired iron shelving for the parts department. Finally, he decided to focus on his farm, planting a huge vegetable garden and raising hogs.

We had no car back then. In fact, Pop Pop never owned or drove a car in his life. We traveled by horse, mule and wagon. We bought our "possibles" at the only grocery store in the area, the Pearl Bargain House. It was located at the foot of Old Jug Bridge in an area called Pearl. Folks bought food, tools, straw brooms and blankets there. They could order what wasn't in stock and pick it up later. We traveled there at night, after working all day on the farm. Cars blasted their horns at us because our only lights were dim oil lanterns. The noise always startled our old horse, Topsy. Pop Pop ignored the cars and mumbled that "the trail was there before the asphalt." In the early 1950s we stayed off the road and took a "hitch ride" with neighbors who needed food. This happened in winter when it was cold and icy, and we were running low on the basics.

Pop Pop and Uncle Elmer planted corn and wheat on about four acres. Work on the farm was difficult. My brother and I had to help when we were living there full-time in the summer. Uncle Elmer and Pop Pop cleaned and cleared about an acre and a half for a vegetable garden. They slopped four hogs twice a day, fed the chickens, and gathered eggs. They split wood for kindling for the wood stove and dumped the fruit jars first thing in the morning.

All of these chores ended up becoming mine and I liked helping with some of the jobs. After spring planting I hated to see the weeds show up. There was little time to play except on rainy days. Sometimes I played in the wagon shop by myself. When other kids showed up to play it was more fun.

My brother Bob and I fetched water and brought it to the house when we were there. We had a 30 foot well outside the kitchen with a hand pump. If it rained the water was too cloudy to drink so we had to haul fresh water from Main's Pond, about 2000 yards away. It was a hilly climb and we spilled the water regularly. We brought the water into the house for drinking and cooking. Uncle Elmer was the cook, and his specialty was brown gravy potato soup, my favorite. We ate as basic as possible.

My brother was older and did not like coming to the farm and being away from his friends in town. Since I was younger, I enjoyed the farm. I started trying things like Brown Mule Chewing Tobacco and collecting pop bottles for deposit. I missed some of my friends from town, but in the country there were other kids I enjoyed.

In the spring, when my brother and I came out to the farm, we helped plant, plow, and weed all through the spring and summer. We fed the hogs, cracked corn twice a day, and cleaned the outhouse. In late summer, we split firewood, kept it dry and stacked on the back porch, and made sure we had water on the porch as well. We kept a push mower for the lawn which we couldn't use until we picked all the black walnuts off the ground.

I also worked on farms around the neighborhood when alfalfa and hay were baled. The bales were loaded on wagons and loose hay was hand raked and loaded on carts. The farms that had tractors loaded the baled hay, and took it to the barns to be stored when it was dry.

The first dollar I was ever paid was $1.50 per day. It cost me $.50 for lunch but I paid it because I was so hungry. I worked at Buddy Fox's Woodrene Farm. We started work at 6 AM and milked the cows at 4 PM. Some days we worked after dark when the corn plants were ready. A load of shucks and cobs had to be unloaded onto the conveyor belt and shot up into the silo whenever they arrived. One day I made three dollars. I needed to be extra careful and not fall on the conveyor and get chopped up like the silage, which happened to others in the county, so I heard. Also, being around the mash could get you dizzy if it started to ferment.

The cool days of fall reminded me of butchering. The goal was to fill the cellar and store food for winter. It was a family affair, and everyone was tuned in with what needed to be done, usually around Thanksgiving. During cold weather we started gathering barrels— the bigger, the better. A big job was pumping water for boiling to shave the hogs after slaughter. If things were not ready before daylight some adults went to their regular jobs.

Pop Pop

When the hogs were butchered, every body part was used. My aunts cooked down the fat to make lard which seasoned a lot of the meat. Some parts of the meat were cold packed in crocks and jars.

After butchering, friends and neighbors bartered with "Doc" for the meat. He was too clever for that because of all the hard work. But if people needed food and couldn't afford to pay that was different. "Doc" would trade shoeing a horse for plowing a garden, or a field, when people were not working.

On a market day, farmers went to town, and sold or traded meat for vegetables, canned fruit, jelly, chestnuts, and English walnuts. The Great Frederick Fairgrounds was another place to sell homemade goods. Local farmers competed for prizes for their outstanding produce. Pop Pop often had huge potatoes and won prizes for them. The women featured their canned jams and vegetables.

We had to make sure we had enough food for the family. Pop Pop always brought a jar of canned cherries that he had stashed away to be used as a special treat for my brother and me. Mom canned the cherries and kept track of what we had. Pop Pop always gave food to folks who helped him cut wood or drag a dead log in from the backwoods for our winter wood pile.

Life was a little simpler after my mother came out to stay in the country. She had just visited during the summer of 1946 and 1947. When she remarried, she finally had access to a car and could spend more time with us in the country.

During the summer months, when my brother and I were helping Pop Pop and Uncle Elmer, it was hard getting used to not having running water and a regular bath. If we had time to go swimming in the summer, by the time we got back home, we were wringing wet with sweat, like before we left.

With no electricity in the house, our lights were oil lamps like you used on horse drawn buggies, and our road wagons smelled like oil or kerosene. Also, we had an outhouse, which wasn't very modern or convenient, especially at night. Cleaning it out once a month was an undesirable task particularly during the hot, humid days of summer.

Pop Pop had electricity put in the house around 1950. He was still having water brought in. It was great that we were modernizing. Pop Pop had wanted Mom to move to the country for years. She and Dad finally agreed to move out there. Sadly, Uncle Elmer took sick and passed away in the early 1950s from stomach cancer. Dad, Bob and I had a lot more responsibilities.

After dinner, when we could relax, Pop Pop often told stories of Uncle Elmer's youthful escapades with "Miss Sophay" (all the ladies had the same name) at the Bluebird Saloon on South Market Street by the firehouse. Pop Pop bowled across the street at the Diamond Bowling Alley while Uncle Elmer was at the saloon. Uncle Joe would show up at an agreed-upon time and drive both of them home.

One tale we heard often starring Pop Pop and Uncle Elmer started out as a joke, but ended up having unpleasant consequences. It was the story of the girl in the box. As the story goes, there was a neighbor girl who teased and embarrassed Elmer and Doc (Pop Pop) repeatedly when they were growing up in Feagaville. The brothers were not troublemakers, but they had about all the teasing they could handle, and had an opportunity to get even. One day when she was in her outside privy next-door, the two boys crept over and slightly tipped the privy over. Pleased with how loud she was hollering and squealing, they let go and the privy tipped completely over. They ran off, but her father had seen them. He hurried over and talked to John, the brothers' dad, and told him what had happened. If the families were going to be good neighbors Elmer and Pop Pop would have to set up the privy back on its blocks. Also, as punishment, the neighbor suggested that Elmer and Pop Pop clean the privy out as often as determined by the neighbor. What started out to be funny was not funny in the end. Pop Pop told this story his whole life. I think he was embarrassed because it was never his intent to cause problems. It was a hard lesson to learn, but kind of a funny story. We always enjoyed the tales of Uncle Elmer and Pop Pop.

(L-R) Me, Arthur "Doc" Ray ("Pop Pop"), Elmer Ray, Bob Loun

5

BROTHER BOB

*M*y earliest memories of my brother and I revolved around ear infections, mumps, measles, and other illnesses. If he caught a bug at school, soon I had it. In 1952 we had our tonsils and adenoids taken out. Right away we both perked up and our health improved.

Counting cars from our third-floor window was a game we enjoyed. The winner was the one who found the most cars of his chosen color. We played board games and card games, but as we grew older we preferred more outdoor activities including fishing and softball. As with most siblings, my brother and I fought a lot. He probably didn't like the responsibility of keeping an eye on me and having me tag along with his friends, but I couldn't do anything about it.

When we were in the city we had the Optimist Club, the YMCA, and the Maryland State School for the Deaf. These places offered us activities, guidance, and a place to play safely. If it weren't for some of these outlets we might not have stayed on the straight and narrow.

In the early years when we went to the country to stay with my grandfather during the summer, our lifestyle was more primitive than in our tiny apartment in the city. We didn't have electricity in the country. Kerosene was the fuel we used. We were fortunate to not have any serious fires. In those days fires were common because without electricity, oil lamps carried from one room to another often tipped over.

Occasionally, we had a chimney fire primarily because we burned greenwood and there was likely a buildup of creosote. The chimney could stay fired up if it was cold, but it wasn't built strong enough to withstand extreme heat, and eventually had to be rebuilt.

Three years was a big age difference growing up, and I think that was why we didn't always get along. The best part of my brother was that, later in life, he became a great asset, introducing me to people, and helping me earn my way into a job. He was responsible for providing several job opportunities when I was in the off-season of baseball. That was the hardest time to get work because of only being available for three months. Most of the jobs I had were "helper jobs" such as working on a meat truck delivering supplies to the A&P store.

Looking back on the episodes of my life from the early years, it was all a challenge. My brother and I were fortunate that my mother had high expectations for our behavior. She kept it real by using scary words, and suggesting that we might go to the orphanage, if we didn't cooperate. That strategy worked well as my brother and I both were good kids most of the time.

6

POTATO CHIP LEAGUE

The Potato Chip League began in the countryside. Three boys started it: Bob, Donnie and a neighbor named Sonny Frye. Sonny was an unpredictable sort, very creative and imaginative. He loved to collect baseball cards and memorize the stats on the backs of the cards. When we broke for lunch, he talked baseball while munching on his potato chips and eating his bologna sandwich. It was the first time I had been exposed to baseball cards and the first time I played the game. Sonny's love of the game was inspiring. We learned baseball terms such as: slaughter, grand slam homerun, shutout, fastball, and no hitter. We talked about some of the greats: Roberto Clemente, Johnny Mize, Joe DiMaggio, Jim Busby, Jim Lemon, and Jackie Robinson.

The three of us played our own game and sometimes had to make a new baseball when we lost our real one. Our homemade baseball was made of masking tape and newspaper. Dad brought home extra rolls of masking tape for us when he was painting around the farmhouse. We wadded the newspaper into a tight ball and wrapped masking tape around it until it was about the size of a real baseball. Our masking tape ball was handy because it was somewhat waterproof. Broom handles were a little hard to find and expensive so we made bats from sumac branches with peeled off bark. Unfortunately, if the "bats" dried out, they cracked, and we had to hunt for new branches.

My brother felt we should develop an organized baseball game with rules and statistics. We named it the Potato Chip League, invented during a lunch break while sharing Sonny's potato chips and talking baseball. As we planned, organized and told our friends about it, the league expanded from our three man team into a "league of its own."

Our statistician was my brother Bob, who created charts that systematically recorded home runs, hits, runs, errors, who was leading, and who was hitting. Bob did a great job with the statistics but there were times when he was working and we had to keep up the recordkeeping. We tried, but couldn't do it as well as Bob. Sonny was fine with the recordkeeping system until he found out he had the lowest batting average, highest earned run average, and the most errors.

Boys from neighboring areas heard about the league. They rode their bicycles over Saturday mornings if we could get together. It was fun to ride bicycles up and down the hills, racing through timothy grass pastures, unless it rained.

Sometimes a little squabble slowed the game down a bit. But we all wanted to play so we worked out any disagreements quickly. We had to play before Pop Pop saw the collection of boys in our front yard and signaled for Bob and me to work around the garden, the corn plants, or the lower 40, as we called it. The boys couldn't stay at our house because the yard wasn't that large when there were so many players. We couldn't play in the fields used for growing wheat, corn or hay either.

Sonny and I loved westerns as much as we loved baseball. When we couldn't play baseball, Sonny and I played with the cards we collected of the cowboys who were famous back in the 1950s. If it rained or we had a game of cowboys, we got on top of the wagon in the blacksmith shop and hung out. We loved the cowboy way: the Silver Screen, Bob Steele, Monte Hale, Johnny Mack Brown, Randolph Scott, Sunset Carson and others. They have stood out as heroes all my life.

Sonny and I had make-believe fights as we sat over pretend card tables and imitated saloon fights. One of us would get shot and bite the dust. We had "fast draw" contests that were realistic when we had caps in our cap guns. We heard who was a faster draw by the sound. We chose sides if other boys joined in one of the play alongs. Most of us chose the names of famous cowboys or Indians.

We had sumac stick horses that we rode on wild horse drives. There was a running brook below the sawmill where we camped. If we shaved all the bark off sumac branches with our pen knives, that would be a white horse and only a good guy could ride that one. A pinto pony had a few shaved spots of white. That's the way we played whatever they taught us on the Silver Screen. Other stars we loved were: Tex Ritter, Buck Jones, and Whip Wilson, who was more famous than most. Fuzzy Q. Jones, Roy Rogers, Gene Autry, Burt Lancaster, and Charlton Heston were names that came later in our growing up days. We still discussed cowboys later even though we didn't play them as we grew older.

All the guys we knew played in the Potato Chip League and also traded baseball bubble gum cards. My brother loved the Cleveland Indians and I loved the New York Yankees. I did not save anything other than Yankee cards at that time.

All those cards ended up at the bottom of a 30 foot well. My mother was trying to fill the well and admitted she threw my cards into it. She had second thoughts but figured the cards didn't have any value. If the cards had been sealed and airtight over the years, there could be a fortune at the bottom of that well! Even my toy guns ended up in that well.

Mom would have kept all the stuff she threw into the well if our roof had not leaked and begun to ruin some of our belongings. So she just threw everything down the well or in the garbage. After we had installed an electric pump and encased the well, we were able to utilize the well and have fresh water once again. We finally got a hot water heater and didn't have to heat water in order to cook and clean.

This was the life we had as kids in the Potato Chip League, playing Silver Screen cowboys, and living on the farm.

7

THREE-FINGERED GLOVE

I am left-handed. When I first played baseball, I had a three-fingered, right-hander's glove. It wasn't a very popular model with most right-handers because the local Sears and Roebuck had better options. This glove had webbing between the fingers and was not that comfortable for right-handers. I couldn't afford to buy a glove for a person who threw the ball with his left hand. With a right-hander's three-fingered glove I could use either hand to catch the ball. I could take the glove off my left hand and throw the ball with my left hand. With me being left-handed, it gave me a chance to catch with my right hand. It worked for me until I could afford a proper glove.

As I recall, I saved money for a glove by trading in bottle caps and soda bottles that I found on the side of the road. I traded them in at the soda pop store and got about a nickel for each bottle and two cents for each cap. The size of the bottle determined how much money I got. It was an easy way to earn money. I was lucky to have survived walking along Route 40 without getting run down by a horse and buggy or a wild cow. Occasionally, an animal would venture into the road and an unsuspecting car would end up overturned in a ditch.

The three-fingered glove was overly padded so I tried to remove some of the stiff padding. I had no success because it was masterfully woven in place. Some kids thought I had something special because it was an unusual glove and they often wanted to try it out. The good players weren't interested. In the end, I learned to catch right-handed in one season, and was probably about nine or ten years old.

This trial and error was part of my learning process. I had to "stick it out" to make it work, and wait until I had the money to buy a glove, receive a worn out glove, or be lucky, and be gifted with a new left-hander's glove.

Me with my three-fingered glove

8

IKE

*D*wight David Eisenhower visited Frederick while he was running for President of the United States. I was 11 years old and so excited to see him. My next-door neighbor, Billy, and I hurried toward the end of the railroad tracks, two blocks from where I lived.

The tracks had been torn up about 25 years earlier but we gathered at the train station with young people on the left-hand side, the bus station side of the street. After a few minutes of clearing the tracks, the General showed up with a wide smile on his face. He was with his wife, Mamie. He took his hat off, even though it was very cold, and waved to the crowd. He wore a full-length heavy overcoat. It sounded like hundreds of people cheering and waving. He remained on the train the whole time he was there. We loved his name, Ike. It sounded so cool, and it seemed like he was always smiling.

One amazing possibility about this visit was that my uncles, who worked on the railroad out of Monrovia, could have been on that train. They would have been in their twenties and thirties and could have met the future President. One uncle was an inspector and he would have been old enough to be my great grandfather. That day was special and I'll never forget it.

In 1964, when I was with the Washington Senators Major League team, President Eisenhower stopped at RFK Stadium and autographed baseballs in the clubhouse for the players, staff, batboys and managers. I still have the ball he autographed.

It was another memorable day.

9

MOUNT CARMEL LITTLE LEAGUE

With the Potato Chip League becoming more popular, neighbors noticed more boys coming to the neighborhood. My brother had us organized so that we had three-man teams and rotations. Winners played the winners of the day's game as we became more competitive. It was occasionally a problem because not everyone was able to play. Some boys opted to go swimming in Linganore Creek, play cowboys, or go fishing. That took the pressure off of our yard.

Mr. Henry Allen Groff, our neighbor and a Deacon at Mount Carmel United Methodist Church, may have noticed that kids were coming from as far as Bartonsville. Mr. Groff and Mr. Fouche, who owned a dairy farm nearby, were instrumental in organizing a church little league. They may have figured if there were so many boys interested in baseball that a league would probably work out pretty well.

Major League Shutout Debut

My hazy recollection is that Mr. Groff, Mr. Harry Baker, Mr. Harry Main, along with Mr. Fouche, met at Mount Carmel United Methodist Church and formed a Little League. Other churches, including the Evangelical, Methodist, Presbyterian and Catholic were also interested. Having a church league might also increase church attendance!

We practiced in the field behind Harry Main's store in the empty parking lot. It was fairly centrally located and always available. Kids came all the way from the Meadow Road area down to New Market. Pretty soon New Market developed their own church league.

It is my belief that kids like me normally would never have gotten a chance to play organized ball even if they were really good and loved to play had these generous, thoughtful men not started this league. We all could play, but none of us knew how good we were. I was so fortunate to be one of those kids.

My shining moment came during a game where Mount Carmel was playing Walkersville. Mr. Harry O. Smith was the manager of Walkersville and also the high school Principal. Mr. Henry Groff was our manager. Walkersville led the game going into the last inning by two runs. I had previously hit two homeruns, one right-handed, and one left-handed, in my debut as a left-handed hitter. The pitcher was instructed to intentionally walk me because they felt they could get the next batter out. Mr. Groff instructed me to make sure the pitcher didn't throw one over the plate. The pitcher threw two pitches for balls. He got too close with the third pitch and I hit a Grand Slam homerun. I raced around the bases so thrilled for my team winning. In my excitement I had to remember not to pass any of the base runners. I was so glad I went for it and didn't hold back. That was my last game in Little League baseball in Mount Carmel and in the Frederick County area. Mr.

Harry O. Smith congratulated me, our manager, and all of our players. I believe that was the championship game. If my memory fails me, I will still remember it as the championship game!

At 13 years old and coming out of Little League baseball, I was honored and thrilled to be selected to the Hershey All-Star team, representing Frederick City, Maryland. I knew that someone had seen me play, and I started to feel pretty good about my future playing baseball. In fact, I always thought Mr. Smith had something to do with my being selected after he saw me play so well against his team. Unfortunately, I found that I had to cancel my selection because my brother was getting married in Albuquerque, New Mexico. That was a huge setback because I wanted to be exposed to city baseball practice and playing, but that wasn't to be. By not going to the game I felt like it alienated me from future selections. I don't know why it would have, but it did, and I never got another invitation.

Ironically, Mr. Harry O. Smith's son, Dick Smith, was a left-handed pitcher who was scouted by the Philadelphia Phillies, and signed a contract with their organization. A Frederick County talent!

At this stage in my life from 1950 to 1953, the people who had an influence, took an interest, or made an impression on me were:

- Mr. Henry Groff, my JV baseball coach and Biology teacher, first person to have me pitch in organized baseball; helped organize church Little League
- Mr. Jack Sharrow, the Frederick Optimist Club President
- Mr. Harry O. Smith, Walkersville High School Principal
- Harry Baker, gave me my first job in the brick industry; first person to comment on how well I played first base; helped organize church Little League

- Mr. William Fouche generously used his pick up truck to transport kids to practice who otherwise had no way to get there; helped organize church Little League
- Mr. Harry Main, his parking lot was our practice field and ballpark; helped organize church Little League

The opportunity to play in this league gave me the start I needed, and the confidence I lacked. I played well and learned how a team works and will never forget it. I am forever grateful for the men who organized that league.

Playing baseball behind Main's store

10

DAYDREAMING

What starts you dreaming as you lay in a hayfield, smelling the timothy grass, looking up at the clouds? Thinking.

Could I be a famous baseball player? Could I be a star and make lots of money?

I ask myself.

What would I do with the money? Retire my mother, build her a new house? Could I play for my favorite team? What would that be like? Have my own baseball card, Sign autographs.

On and on and on.

Summers filled with dreams at nine, ten, and eleven years old.

Reality awakens me. It could never happen.

11

CHALLENGES

As if my childhood was not disruptive enough having been optioned out to Brunswick, I was learning more about things to do in the city, but we lived in a dangerous section of town. Both playtime and early school days had challenges from ages 5 to 13.

An area called Cannon Hill, located near the train station, was off-limits to us kids because it was unsafe. There was a jagged, rugged limestone cliff on the edge of the hill. Groups of men camped out at the bottom of the hill where they had some privacy from the residents. They had jumped off the train, knapsacks on their backs, before the train pulled all the way into the train yard. Their campfires alerted us when they were in town. They used the nearby town creek for bathing and washing clothing. I heard that some of them stayed in town for days and did odd jobs for money. A lot of them spent time drinking whiskey, I was told.

It was not an area that kids should play in, but it was a cool hill to explore. There was a cave on Cannon Hill that provided a great shelter on rainy days. On one occasion when I was about six years old and by myself, I was playing on Cannon Hill. A couple of older, larger kids threatened to push me over the cliff. I was terrified and too small to defend myself. Luckily, two brothers, coincidentally named Bobby and Donnie, came along and chased them away. I think our names always connected Bob and me with the brothers.

Since my birthday was in November, I was always young for my school year. In fact, my first school experience was first grade. That was not a good situation for a boy to be the youngest, or among the youngest, in the class. Plus, I was always one of the smallest in the class until high school. Later in life, one of my observant high school classmates told me that I should have started school later to maximize my ability.

Keeping up with my disruptive lifestyle, I attended three different schools before I reached high school. On one occasion, while a friend and I were walking home from Washington Street School, we were waiting for the light to change. We had just made a penny candy purchase—black licorice, my favorite. As we waited at the light, a younger and smaller boy stood with us and bragged that he could make it to the other side of the street even though cars were moving in both directions. As he darted off, a dump truck that had been out of his view hit him. It flung him up in the air. We didn't see him land, but wanted to believe he broke away. We were shocked and immediately raced a block to my apartment. We heard the ambulance arrive and wanted to return to the scene of the accident but were too afraid. It was a dangerous lesson for us, and one we never would forget.

On the Washington Street School grounds, Mayor Don Rice allowed his son to let me ride his bicycle. We were both about six or seven years old and learned to ride a bicycle at the same time. It was the first time I had been on a bicycle and I knew that I desperately wanted one after that. Ten years later, I played baseball against his boys, who were in DeMolay, another youth organization.

When we lived in town during my elementary school years, we did not have our own car. Uncle Joe's car, which was mostly rusted out, was our best mode of transportation if we needed to go somewhere, but, we had to be on his schedule. Once I was caught in his car in the dead of winter outside of one of his favorite watering holes. I had to wait in the car and I remember how cold and painful that night was. Gusting snow blew up through the floorboards and I was freezing. I didn't complain though, because it was my only way to get around.

When I was at Parkway school in fourth and fifth grade, I met Donnie Keller. His father, Charlie "King Kong" Keller had played thirteen years with the Major League New York Yankees. I really liked a baseball glove Donnie had which he let me use. I really didn't want to give it back to him because it was soft and looked so nice. He said his father gave it to him. Maybe it was the one his father had used when he was in professional baseball.

I remember my teacher, Mrs. Hatcher, had half fourth graders and half fifth graders the same year. Each group sat on a different side of the room. I had her for two years, so I sat on the left side one year and the right side the next year. She was a very optimistic teacher and I enjoyed my years with her. She complimented me on my writing style and encouraged me to write a weekly article for the school newspaper. 70 years later, I finally started writing again. Playing softball at recess at Parkway was popular, but tricky. If the ball got away, we could not chase it into the road. After my years at Parkway, we moved to the country and walking to school was not an option.

Major League Shutout Debut

Attending Elm Street School in seventh and eighth grades involved riding the bus from the country to town. I remember a sexy-looking Miss Thomas, my teacher. Most of the guys found her so attractive we had difficulty getting out of our seats at the end of class. We waited until most of the students were out of the room, and with looks of discomfort, we screened ourselves with our books as we scurried out of class. Mr. Griffin, another teacher, had greenish hair. I heard he was a great athlete, who swam before school every day, which explained the green hair.

Adjusting to being in the country instead of living in town was challenging. I enjoyed walking to school and being near our apartment in town. The longer bus ride meant we could not stay after school for sports or clubs. We couldn't stay in town for the weekends to participate in town activities. It was a lot of change.

12

BING

𝓑ing was great at organizing the local boys before there was an Optimist Club. He was my brother's age and was looked up to by all the kids in the neighborhood. He found the biggest backyards he could put together to create a football field. We played tackle football with no shoulder pads or helmets. This was before the corn plant folded and the park became available across from South Street. Every Saturday we beat each other up pretty badly. After work on summer evenings we played in Bing Keeney's big backyard with Snookie Unglenbauer, Flicker Bear, Bing, and my brother. Bing always looked out for us in case we were playing too rough. He was always encouraging us to try harder.

Bing went on to play for the Frederick Falcons, a semi-pro football team that developed in Frederick. I think he was the main organizer and the person who got the sponsors. There was a five or six team league with two teams in Hagerstown and one team in Frederick. Bing was eventually inducted into the Alvin G. Quinn

Sports Hall of Fame and the Semi-Pro Football Hall of Fame. He deserved it because he was a real go-getter when it came to putting teams together and being "the leader of the pack."

Bing organized a Turkey Bowl football game when I was a young teen that took place around Thanksgiving in Baker Park. I heard that other teams wanted to play even though there were no helmets or shoulder pads. I remember trying to throw a block and I was too young to be doing it but I did it anyway and the opponents ran over me. Bing told them to get up and encouraged me to keep standing. I continued to play, but I think the guys were worried about me being overrun. We tried to block out everyone.

After my first year in professional baseball, I played a couple of softball teams in Baker Park one weekend. They were playing slow pitch and I remember throwing the ball in from left field. It was probably the hardest I ever threw a softball, but I remember that was at the end of my involvement with any of the local sports teams in Frederick until I came back after being released in 1969. At the time I had a nice reunion with Bing.

Bing always came to play. He could ring your "bell."

13

OPTIMIST CLUB

One of the best opportunities I ever had was to be part of the Optimist Club. It was important in my development, even though it wasn't heavy-handed. The boys were taught to respect the rules of the club, take care of the equipment, clean up behind ourselves, and mostly, have fun.

The organized games of flag football, King of the Mountain, kickball, softball and dodgeball taught us sportsmanship and teamwork. We played all kinds of board games and card games. One of my favorite games was Battleship. The strategy was fun to plan and I was a pretty good player. Swimming, hiking in the mountains, and camping overnight were wonderful experiences. On any given day, there were about 50 kids, ages 9 to about 16, who showed up and enjoyed the variety of activities. Rain or shine, we had a place to go to meet our friends. Exposure to so many activities helped build self-confidence and character. This group helped mold me, as I grew older, into the productive, law-abiding, self-confident, and successful adult that I became.

The president of the club, John Jack Sharrow, was also my Sunday School teacher. In addition to Bible stories, news stories, human interest stories, and life stories, he taught us to respect the police, firemen and ladies. He taught us to be gentlemen. He was a good listener, was patient, and answered our questions.

One gentleman I would like to acknowledge was a man by the name of Lease Bussard. We did not know him well, but we needed his building. It provided the space for the club as long as it was a viable, working club. I think the Optimist Club eventually outgrew the location on South Street. Mr. Bussard was a godsend to us because there were at least a dozen kids, including myself, who would use the facility whenever it was available. I remember Bing Keeney, Snookie Unglebauer, Philip Welty, Billy Hurt, Johnny Barber, George May Junior, Charley Hoffman, Charlie Hahn, Bill Stup, and Lester Boyle. Some of them were good friends with my brother also.

My brother was a junior president and the 16-year-old boxing champ. He was also great at making speeches and frequently entered oratorical contests until we moved to the country. He attended competitions where he had to first win in town. If he won he would travel to other cities such as Richmond, Alexandria, and Arlington, Virginia, where other boys' clubs would meet for competitions. He was fortunate enough to place in every competition he entered and was awarded several first place finishes. His good friend and competitor was Lester Boyle. They brought out the best in each other. Everyone thought Bob's future would be in politics, but that did not pan out.

I stepped up to be the 12 and 13-year-old boxing champ. In one unfortunate situation, someone had the less than brilliant idea to have my brother, the sixteen year old champion, box me. I was knocked out in the first round with two shots to my nose. I could see up, but not down, after a quick ending to the mismatched competition.

So lucky to have been part of the Optimist Club. Safe haven. Friends. Activities.

14

TRYOUTS

*O*verly confident? In seventh and eighth grade I tried out for a variety of clubs, with mixed success.

I enjoyed music and thought I had rhythm, so I decided to try out for the band. The five dollar drum I bought at a country auction was a weird-looking snare drum, but sounded good when I played it. The kids got a kick out of it because they had never seen anything like it anywhere. I thought it would be easy to carry in the marching band. However, it was missing the stand and shoulder straps. Reading sheet music rapidly was also a challenge I needed time to overcome. Lessons were too expensive and not an option. Sadly, I did not make the cut.

Glee Club was my next attempt to include music in my life at school. The music teacher apparently did not agree and gently suggested I try out for Drama Class instead. Perfect! I hadn't thought about Drama, but I had years of experience portraying various cowboys of the Silver Screen. I auditioned for a part in a play, and was so excited when I was chosen! I only had one line, but it was a very important character. My one line was, "Yes, indeed I was. I helped free Argentina from the Spanish rule."

The teacher, Miss Thomas, tried to teach me an appropriate Spanish accent. (Was I focused too much on the lovely Miss Thomas?) She patiently went over the line repeatedly, but I could not get the feel of the delivery. Here I was, San Martin, a Spanish general and hero in Argentina. I practiced but never felt that my San Martin was believable. My time in Drama Club was brief.

Storytelling sounded like a venture I could handle as I fancied myself a pretty good storyteller. At least that's what they told me back on the farm. In one story, I was able to describe a terrible fight in my front yard on the farm between my love, Lassie dog, and an unwanted visitor, a black and white little fellow, who had a peculiar odor about him. I told the story like this:

> *I got up one morning and was getting ready for school, and sure enough, there was a ruckus in the backyard. Our dog Dottie, fearless as she was, had taken on a skunk who had no business in the yard. She knew it and tried to scare the little guy with her barking. The skunk swatted her and reached to hook her in the nose. Eventually the skunk was successful and hooked his paw onto her nose. What a horrible sight.*
>
> *I hurriedly put on my pea coat to get outside to help because Dottie was yelping and backing up in circles, trying to shake that wild critter off. She finally made one quick snap. Taking all the pain, she jumped on that varmint and strangled it. That was the end of Mr. Skunk. I was trying to distract the skunk, but the damage was already done.*

The school bus was coming down the hill, picking up kids along the way. I grabbed my books and raced. I jumped on the crowded bus, not knowing that the kids were smelling the presence of a skunk. I never thought it was me. I thought it was someone else. Four miles later we drove up to Elm Street School. Everyone got out and went to their classrooms.

I went to the cloak room and hung up my beautiful new pea coat. Well, you can imagine what the classroom was experiencing with my presence. The teacher suggested the class take an early recess. That was really out of character for her. She asked for Donald to stay behind. That was me! She took me to the cloak room where the pea coat was hanging all by itself. Guilty as charged.

There was not much I could do about it because I was miles from home and she wasn't going to put me back in class. Instead, I was assigned to clean up papers around the schoolyard until the end of class which was the rest of the day. I remained outside until the bus arrived. That was the only way I could get home. My pea coat was still full of skunk smell. The kids on the bus were all over me with agitating comments.

Those things just happen to everybody and the kids should have rolled along with it. It was an awful story and an awful thing to put people through and I knew that. If I had owned another coat I would have changed. My mother would have rescued me had she been available but she was already at work, and my grandfather was oblivious to the whole episode. End of story.

The sad part was, it was a true story. I'm not sure if I ever wore that coat again.

15

AN UNTIMELY SETBACK

Some teachers know how to get the best out of children. Some teachers get a kick out of making kids laugh at each other. I was lucky to have mostly kind, caring and supportive adults in my life, including teachers.

One of my favorite learning experiences was when we studied the Civil War. The class had a student created mural that extended around the entire room with drawings of events that occurred during the Civil War. It was special to learn how involved our town, Frederick, was in the war. I recall learning that when General Lee's map was found, Union troops had time to slow down the Confederate army that was advancing toward Gettysburg, and disaster.

I had one memorable teacher who singled me out. I was called on in class because it looked like I did not know the answer to a question. Apparently, I had a stupid look on my face, according to the teacher. I was called to the front of the room, where the teacher confirmed that I did not know the answer, and berated me with more questions that I could not answer. The teacher persisted unmercifully until I began to cry in front of the class. Not a good look for an adolescent boy.

When I went back to my seat, little did the teacher know that that humiliation was a major setback in my effort to develop self-confidence and a positive attitude. I lost motivation to work in the class for the rest of the year. The embarrassment and hurt festered for a long time. I'm not sure whether the teacher liked or disliked me, but, I have not forgotten that incident, and how long it took me to recover from it. I do recall consoling comments and comforting pats on the back made by friends of mine after class.

As I reminisce at age 83, the many positive influences I was fortunate enough to have had far outweighed the few negative ones, and for that I am grateful.

16

TWO-WHEELED CONVERTIBLE

*L*iving in the country and trying to get to baseball practice was an issue of transportation. My bicycle enabled me to have more opportunities since Mom, Dad and Bob were usually working.

The route was familiar because I had walked to the farms when I worked on them. My route was to go to Ijamsville Road and Richie's Farm from my home on Meadow Road. Working on the farms was great because I picked up extra money and bought the little doodads that grown-up boys started to need like pen knives and straw hats. A baseball hat at that time cost a buck and a half and that was a lot of money.

A home for the elderly was on my bicycle route. It was creepy because of the rumors about the "bottomless" quarry that was in front of the home. Rumor had it that a train had left the tracks and one unrecovered car was buried at the bottom of that quarry. If we asked adults about the rumors they agreed that they heard the stories, but added that no one ever investigated. An unsolved mystery.

The Ijamsville ball diamond was my destination on my bicycle. This area was also an equestrian exercise area. Attention paid to the droppings scattered around the outfield was essential. Before practice we cleaned up a bit so we didn't have to do a double shuffle over the top of horse manure to catch a fly ball that was hit during batting practice.

Practice was not attended by many of the older players because they worked full time. Practice was set late enough for the guys to get there after work but then they ran into a daylight problem. Once summer came it was better. Spring was tough because it rained often. After a big shower the ballpark had a mud infield that had to be dredged, spruced up, and raked. We had a sand pile and everything we needed to make the mound tight. I don't remember working on the mound, but I learned as a professional how to shape one properly.

At practices the left-handers hit first and all the right-handers hit next. Therefore, we didn't have everybody spread out. There weren't that many of us to shag fly balls, but that was the beginning of an education. We hadn't done that in Little League because we didn't have the space. We practiced at home. Nine Grounders was a popular game. In the game, each player hit three fly balls and nine grounders. The next guy up hit the same. We rotated out of left field. We didn't know what the game Pepper was at that time, but later that became the exercise for our reflexes.

After practice I dreaded the ride home because of darkness. A bike rider would be difficult to see on the moonlit back roads. One guy had a pick up truck and offered to drive several of us home. We put our bikes in the back of his pick up truck. It happened occasionally at first, and was appreciated, except it put him out of his way. He never complained. It was one of those things guys did as part of a team. Even so, I didn't want to bother him unless I could reciprocate somehow.

    The best thing for me was to leave a bit early from practice and ride home before dark. When my brother came to practice he drove the car and I didn't have to worry about darkness. Surprisingly, as much as I loved my two-wheeled convertible and depended on it, I don't recall my brother having a bicycle of his own.

17

WAKE UP CALL

*I*n life there are a couple of things that run together. When someone has tried to intimidate you, you recognize it and may give it back in full measure. The other thing is, don't ever get beaten because you didn't throw, or give your best stuff. I take this back to high school days when the freshman class was trying out for the JV football team. I was pretty good in my first football scrimmage.

I was the offensive and defensive tight end. I tried to sniff out the plays as well as I could. I was feeling very comfortable with my play and confident that I had a decent chance to make the team. I really wanted to try to be a good teammate and make the first team. It looked like I was well on my way when there was an incident that shook me up.

During a defensive play that went to the right, my right, as I was the tight end, I came in from the left side. An offensive running back I didn't see rushed toward me, and took me out.

Unfortunately for me, the player was a guy who I really wanted to get to know, and be friends with. I thought we could win ball games together. It kind of set me back that he would pull a particular hit to take me out of a play that I was already out of because the play went the other way. I was in the backfield, and it would have been chasing down the left running back, but the right running back had peeled off and rattled my chain. My feelings and pride were hurt. I felt like I had done my best and the viciousness or lack of concern for my good health kind of got in the way of that play. In the end, however, he did the right thing because I started watching my backside. Nice play, Davy!

It took a little edge off my intuitiveness because I had not played organized football in any capacity. I was a ninth grade freshman and learning to play was part of the game. Well, there was a lesson that I learned. No matter which side of the ball I was on, I had to give it all up and recognize that my opponent was trying to make himself look good too.

I credit the running back on the other team because he reminded me:

> *Take the good with the bad and give the best you have always and don't let up because that's when you get injured.*

18

CLOSE ENCOUNTERS

My first memorable injury occurred in Brunswick during my "optioned out" years when I was about four years old. It resulted in the loss of use of the first joint of my right index finger. I cut it while peeling a potato and damaged the tendon to the point where I could not bend the finger past the first joint. When my finger was bandaged it was stiff and stuck out like my very own cowboy gun; probably the only good thing about the injury! I recall that surgery would have been expensive so I had to live with not being able to bend the first joint for the rest of my life. In the winter that finger became extremely cold as it was more sensitive to temperature changes. It also had several infections.

On the farm we wore sneakers in the blacksmith and carpentry shops. My brother and I invariably stepped on nails that penetrated our sneakers, and caused infections. Porter's Liniment and Watkins Salve were our "go to" medicines. Each one pulled the poison or rust fragments from the bottoms of our feet. Heavier shoes or boots would have been more appropriate, but they were expensive, and it was summer.

My third significant injury occurred while engaging in Sir Lancelot sword fighting with my neighbor, Sonny. While in a "fight for survival" with our sumac wood sticks, he accidentally sliced me right below my right eye. I never had any stitches but probably should have had stitches. I'm sure we could not afford the medical bills. That was the end of sword fighting for us.

On another occasion, my friend JB, and I, were engrossed in a rock fight. We were in the backyard of the Bright Spot Soda Fountain on South Market Street next to the train station. JB fired a rock and nailed me to the right of my right eye. It didn't break anything except the skin, but it bled profusely which terrified us. That was a close call that could have had a profound effect on my future.

The next major injury occurred when I was bounding over a ramp on my bicycle and accidentally caught the top edge of the ramp which dumped me on the ground. I lay there in pain, hardly moving until my brother helped me get up. I rested on the couch the rest of the day hoping the pain would subside. The following day, the doctor determined that I had broken my collarbone. After a full few tugs and pulls, my collarbone was reset, and I was on my way.

Another memorable injury occurred when a meat hook that we used for butchering was thrown into my left arm. It landed near my elbow and was subsequently pulled out. That was scary because it was my left arm, and I am left-handed. It took a while to heal, but there were no lingering problems. Fortunately, no further problems resulted from that incident. Watkins Salve saved the day.

The first time I brought my uniform home from JV football practice my brother wanted to wear my shoulder pads. I had already broken my collarbone once and needed to be careful. As we were playing, I tripped at the line of scrimmage and fell again on my shoulder, breaking my right collarbone for the second time. Our doctor issued a warning that a third break might require surgery, and the insertion of a metal pin, which did not sound good to a 13-year old, aspiring football player. Additionally, my mother refused to sign any more waivers for me to play football in school. I had no opportunity to play except intramural football which I did because I could throw the ball 50 yards or more. That was the end of my football endeavors, and also most of my injuries.

Regarding high school football, I couldn't stand to attend the games. I was a sophomore, watching the varsity play and remembered how well I had played in the tryout for JV. It was disappointing to be left out. I knew I was a player. Even when Coach Hummel asked me to come to practice and told me he had special shoulder pads that would protect my shoulder and wanted me to kick because he had seen me kicking during intramurals, my mother still would not sign.

Instead, I sold hotdogs and drinks throughout the stands during my early high school days along with my brother. If we earned any money we donated it to the Optimist Club. Since we didn't keep our tips, we were offered some leftover hotdogs after the game, which we enjoyed. I still love hotdogs today!

During the 9 years that I played professional baseball there were several injuries, but they were all recoverable. I call it character building. As an adult I have had two rotator cuff surgeries and two hip replacements. Just a few minor inconveniences along the way!

19

WILD AS A KILLDEER

After recuperating from a broken collarbone, I ventured out to play JV baseball in 1955 for my former Little League coach, Henry Allen Groff. He was both my biology teacher and my JV baseball coach.

During that spring training freshman year in JV baseball, I pitched my first and last high school game against our Frederick High School varsity team in a practice game. The varsity squad were the Frederick County superstars and had a great record. Players I recall on that team were Don Brown, Frank Martz, Charlie Keller lll, Donnie Keller, and Bucky Summers. As I recall, the varsity Frederick High School baseball team was coached by Hal Keller, who was my Business Law teacher. In the lone practice game where I was asked to pitch by Mr. Groff, I struck out a few, grazed a few, but pitched very well. No runs, no hits, no errors. Students who saw or heard about the game complimented me in the hallways at school and congratulated me on how well

I pitched. I was proud of myself. If the students noticed, it would seem that a coach would have noticed that I had a live arm, and was full of piss and vinegar. Anybody home?

I worked out conscientiously that season with the JV team. We played intrasquad games where I was pitching as wild as a killdeer. I was getting people out even though I thumped a few during batting practices. If I drove in seven runs, I ended up walking and hitting people and letting them score. After a few outings, I hated hitting my teammates with my wild pitches, and did not want to pitch.

A pitcher from the Baltimore Orioles organization was brought in and wanted to see me throw. I threw, and he urged me to throw harder. I threw harder and he kept encouraging me to put more into it. He told me to reach back like I was going to pick up a handful of grass. It felt good, so I went after it, and threw the ball about 20 feet over the catcher's head! Finally, I got the idea of throwing hard. I realized I could throw a lot harder and that might benefit me on the field, throwing in to the cut off man. It might have also suggested I could pitch. That first year was not very impressive other than driving in runs. I was playing outfield, and occasionally, first base.

My second year of JV baseball I was pretty sure I would have a good year with the bat. I expected to play outfield and first base because no one was asking me to pitch. Bob Moss was the only real pitcher they had on the varsity team and he was very good. He wasn't overpowering, but he was very consistent. I don't remember any highlights from the year when I reflect on it. During this time in the city, I was also playing in the adult Heart of Maryland League when I stayed in the country.

My junior year in high school I was on the varsity team. I was pretty good with the bat, but I played in the outfield. I felt good out there but I was a little wild. The coaches worried I might throw the ball through the infield so they ended up having me play first base. Charlie Keller II, God bless his soul, hit me ground balls for practice at first base as long as I could stand up. He really worked me over by hitting me so many balls, and being grateful and wanting to impress him, I was determined to catch them all. I got pretty comfortable at first base, liked it, and played it all year. I ended up hitting around .300 in high school which was not that impressive. Again, I don't recall being asked to be on the pitching staff in my high school.

My senior year I played good baseball, nothing flashy, but I made the plays. I tried to learn as much as I could. I may have played the outfield a few times, but I was mostly on first base. I really worked on stretching and knocking the ball down and generally learning how to play infield. If it was a wild throw by "Ooo Lay" Frankie Martz at third, or if Donnie Keller at shortstop, went in the hole and came up, I had to get the out. The fielding went well. I may have hit some triples and doubles, and drove in a few runs, but nothing to write home about that season. Coach Keller was not available senior year as he had been hired as manager of Washington's Rookie League team in Nebraska. He would return as the Senators' Assistant Farm Director one year later, and our paths would cross significantly.

I remember one Charlotte Hall High School game my senior year. We were behind, and the bases were loaded. I hit a homerun over the dressing room on the far side of right field. I was a hero for a moment on a team I never felt a part of. I think that was because I never got a chance to socialize with the players off the field. It wasn't a team thing. It was just that we were on the field together. For that day I felt good, a member of the team, and appreciated all the kind words from the players. That game was the best memory of my high school baseball career.

20

FOUL BALL

Trying to make first team varsity basketball was something I realized a bit late was not a possibility. Some of the city boys had played together for years and the second team that was on that squad was backed up by the JV Club. More of those guys were going to get a chance to play if the game got out of control. It knocked me right out of the varsity for two years. I had hoped to play there but it didn't discourage me.

In the country we had a basket nailed up against the side of the barn. When it was wet and rainy, and, of course, in the fall and winter, the ground was sloppy with mud. The basket was below the pigpen yard which had to be kept wet because the hogs slept in it. Eventually, my brother and I moved the basket close to the house. We were trying to be upwind of the outhouse and downwind of the chicken house. It was a predicament.

Major League Shutout Debut

There are certain shots in basketball that you have to take and they're usually corner shots that make the difference in a 1-3-1 zone. So those are the shots I worked on day and night.

The barnyard was not exactly the best setup for those shots because the ground sloped downhill so when I took a shot, I was on a higher slope shooting downhill to the basket, and when I was downhill, I was shooting uphill. The difference was about 3 to 4 feet. The barnyard, pigpen, chicken house, outhouse, blacksmith shop, wagon shop, and chicken yard were full of mud, water, and hogs, depending on the time of year. Often roofing nails would poke through the wood and put a hole in the balls if we shot them too high. Sometimes we had to dribble with a bicycle patch or an inner tube patch where there were holes in the ball, and it would make a flap, flap, flap sound, but we would be able to somehow keep it in the air. We regularly stepped on nails on the barn floor. It worked for a while to play this way.

Moonlight was our only light source providing plenty of distracting shadows. Bats passing through at night occasionally met with a shock when hit "accidentally." I would dribble and shoot, dribble and shoot, over and over again, sometimes with muddy hands when the ground was wet. There was a backboard and I did not want a muddy ball so I kept the ball moving as much as possible. In any case, I worked at it and got the shots down consistently. The main shot on the 1-3-1 zone offense against zone defense is where they don't shift fast enough. You take the shot from the corner and everyone's following up, but if they pick you up, you can drive by them. I took those shots when I could and followed up just like you are supposed to do. My percentage went up. I thought I had a real chance to make the team because I outmaneuvered my competition regularly. However, that was not going to happen. It just hardened me for the county varsity team where I was a starter. It was good, but not what I worked for, and wanted.

I played county varsity basketball for two years but never got a chance with the high school varsity club and that was disappointing. There was something magical about just being on the floor of the gymnasium, packed with students going crazy. It was special when you came out on the floor and they played the school song, and a good feeling of school pride. I never got to enjoy it as a team member.

The county varsity was primarily for kids to get out of one class during the day to take in the game or get the afternoon off to play our game. We didn't draw any crowds. It wasn't the magic the varsity enjoyed. I still miss the surge of adrenaline that basketball brought and what it meant to be trying to make the team. I felt like a nobody. I guess at that time it felt like we were discriminated against because we were from the country. What mattered was if you were trying to make the varsity club look bad, and that happened regularly because we practiced against them every night, except game night. That was taken on a personal basis, but mostly in basketball, in my opinion.

The county varsity team did have some good luck at one particular time when we were playing Walkersville High School and future Philadelphia Philly, Dick Smith, was the crowd pleaser out of Walkersville. At that time Walkersville was a county team because they didn't have a large high school. They also drew from a wide area so they had some pretty good players. They had to keep a portion of seats open for those guys. Smith brought good stuff every time he played. That was a 1 on 1 for me and I wasn't giving him anything. He didn't like that a whole lot and neither did the officials. It was the first quarter and I had seven points already and was dominating. It didn't take long before I was conveniently sitting on the bench for the rest of the game. I will agree that I committed four out of the five fouls.

I just wanted to be part of the varsity team because I was convinced I earned it. I believed no one worked as hard as I did.

21

A FLICKERING STAR

When I aged out of Little League, I played in the Heart of Maryland League, which I did all through high school during the summer, and whenever I could. It was an adult baseball league in the county and they played during March, April and May. Unfortunately, when I was 14, I mostly sat on the bench because I was one of the youngest players. At age 15, I had the opportunity to play first base and outfield. It was great to have a chance to play baseball at least one day a week. It was also nice having my brother on the same team.

Major League Shutout Debut

Bob and I played together in the Heart of Maryland adult league

The adult league seldom had practice games which I always wondered about. It was hard to get adults to show up for games, much less practice, so we were relegated to playing only on Sunday. Those games never had a doubleheader that I can recall, and it was very limited league play. The first night game I ever played was in Germantown and I found it exciting to play under the lights.

We did get some practice games at the field that we played on in Ijamsville with the Heart of Maryland League and the Maryland State League. The best players from the city and county were in the Maryland State League and had more experience. With our team, if you practiced you played, but with the state team, the best players always seemed to be the ones who played.

A Flickering Star

Players began coming out of town and taking all the positions on the state ball club, and basically getting free meals or free food after every workout because they were supported by two gentlemen from Baltimore, Judge Morelan and Mr. Smith. Smith really loved the game of baseball and wanted his son to play. My buddy, Roy Hiltner, kept me informed as to how that would pan out. It worked well because Judge Morelan treated me to a delicious lunch of fresh ham, gravy, and mashed potatoes at the Francis Scott Key Hotel. He tried to coax me over to his ball club. He thought I was good enough to play there and they were looking to bolster their image.

It was a separation I just couldn't make because of the friendships I had formed with the guys in the Heart of Maryland League. The Hiltner twins, Harold "Tootie" Hargett, and I buddied up. Tootie helped organize a baseball team in the Heart of Maryland league. Some of the other players were Jim Kelly, Bink Myers, Gene Geisler, Bob and George Ed Grubbs, Donnie and Bill Wilcom, and Clark Castle. My baseball interest continued as I performed well even though I was younger than most of the players.

We washed cars for Tootie's Texaco station on East Patrick Street across from the Potomac Edison Company. Gasoline was $.24 a gallon. We sat around talking about our ball games and practices, girls, and cars. It was a nice friendly group. I was a dimly lit "flickering star" at the time.

Roy never thought much about the large state team, but he and his twin brother, Ray, did take care of the field for them by cutting the grass before every Sunday game. That enabled us to use the field also. It was a business agreement with Judge Morelan and Mr. Smith. Once in a while, we were invited to practice with them or meet at Jug Bridge Inn for an occasional hamburger. Ours was a friendship more than baseball.

Roy had gotten me my first real job as a sophomore in high school. It was my first real job off the farm, at age 16, making $1.00 per hour, working for a Janitorial Product Company called Fisher Lang, Inc. I had that job through high school with Roy. We were breaking down 55 gallon drums of wax and mixing up cleaning products that were used in the schools in Frederick County and throughout Southern Maryland.

Mom and me at my Frederick High School graduation, 1958

After high school, I moved to the William D. Bowers Lumber Company building prefabricated houses. I played baseball as time allowed. Bowers Lumber Company was conveniently located by the railroad tracks where the lumber could easily be unloaded. I hauled lumber all over the county in the form of cabinets and other furniture. Being competitive, I always wanted to see if I could get back to the warehouse faster than the rest of the crew when I delivered a load. Later the company expanded to Sixth Street which was the former Frederick Iron and Steel Warehouse and old silo building.

Prefabricated housing and roof truss systems were new to the building industry at the time and certainly made construction quicker and more economical. The Bowers Lumber Company was on the ground floor of these home building methods that could churn out homes quickly. Rosehill, Clover Hill and the southeastern part of Frederick grew rapidly as a result during 1958-1960s.

Definitely a highlight of my week was my opportunity to play baseball. Little did I know that my flickering star was soon going to get much brighter.

22

STAY ON THE MOUND

Around this time, I met a guy named Ralph "Tuck" Snyder. He was the manager of our baseball team in Buckeystown with the Tri-County Adult League. The Heart of Maryland League eventually dissolved, and most of the players joined the larger Tri-County League.

It was while I was playing with Tuck Snyder that he had me pitch one game when our pitcher, "Tootie" Hargett, was not feeling well. It was blazing hot and I think Tootie had a sun stroke. Someone had to pitch and we didn't have any other pitchers. I always played first base or outfield. Can you imagine, because I was closest to the pitcher's mound, I became the pitcher? When you get the opportunity, as I did, I took full advantage of it, and struck out 18 batters in 6 ⅔ innings that day.

That brought some new interest my way. When I got home, I found a congratulatory telegram. I had a phone call from

Major League Shutout Debut

Joe Price, a scout with the Baltimore Orioles organization. An invitation to a tryout camp the Orioles were hosting was offered. I began imagining the reality of my childhood dream of becoming a professional baseball player. I embraced the possibilities, 100%.

Joe Price was the first guy to come to our practice after I had struck out 18 guys. He said, "If you want to play professional ball you're going to have to stay on the mound and pitch."

That is all I needed to hear. My focus changed immediately.

Years before I met Tuck, he had given up an opportunity to go to Washington DC in a white, chauffeured Cadillac, and try out with the Washington Senators. He had just finished his work with the railroad, and had two weeks pay in his hand.

His mother said, "A bird in the hand is better than two in the bush."

She discouraged him from going, so he never played professional baseball and always regretted it. He eventually went into the Army and injured his arm. He was a "big brute," but a good man. He had a heart of gold, and did what he said he would do. He told me that if I ever had a chance to play professional baseball, he would make himself as available as possible to help me.

He told me, "I'll make sure I take you to wherever you need to play and whatever it takes."

I knew I could count on him.

Stay on the Mound

*Manager Ralph "Tuck" Snyder (left) and me
at my Baltimore Orioles tryout*
Photo Credit: *Frederick News-Post*

    Tuck accompanied me to the tryout in Hagerstown. We dressed in suits to look as professional as possible. Upon arrival, I changed into my spotless Buckeystown uniform, ready to see what the future held for me. At the Hagerstown camp I played first base all day. There seemed to be just two of us the camp was interested in: Kenny Eves and myself. Kenny waited around all day and finally got to pitch. The problem was that the Baltimore Orioles coaches discovered that their camp had a scout from the Philadelphia Phillies in it. They didn't want the scout to see Kenny or myself, so they intentionally held us back most of the day. It was a blazing 90 degrees day in July. Finally, we pitched, and the Orioles wanted me to sign the very next day.

Philly's scout, Jim Brinkley, told my manager, Tuck, not to let me sign anything. Brinkley felt there was some bonus money out there, maybe as much as $25,000. He said I should move onto another camp to try out for the Philadelphia Phillies in two weeks.

Things were developing fast.

Within one week the interest in this string bean left-hander was getting pretty serious. After the tryout in Hagerstown, Joe Price insisted I come down to Memorial Stadium and play against the East Coast Champions of Baltimore, the Leones. They were nationally ranked. I had a successful outing, striking out most of the batters I faced. Orioles scout and Leonie's manager, Walter Youse, called me, and said I should report to Bluefield, West Virginia, if I wanted to play. He attached a monthly salary offer if I made the team.

After the Orioles tryout camp, Phillies owner, Mr. Carpenter, had planned to fly to Walkersville, but his schedule must have changed because he never arrived. Instead, the next day, Tuck and I went to the Phillies camp in Delaware. There was a lot of confusion because their camp was wide open. The overwhelmed coaches spent most of the time taking down names and didn't really know who was whom. The offer for out-of-towners was $250 a month and no reimbursement expenses. The scouts were interested only in the players they brought, and Jim Brinkley told us he wasn't going to be there. Therefore, no advocate for me. That was a total waste of a weekend.

Stay on the Mound

Dr. Thomas Allen, my dentist, called Coach Jackson at the University of Maryland. Coach Jackson wanted me to come to the school and consider what the school might offer if I was interested. The meeting was set for February 11. A huge blizzard kept me off the hazardous roads. The telegram I sent saying I couldn't get there was never answered. That meeting was never rescheduled.

The winter was long. I didn't want to lose my only shot at professional baseball. Tuck suggested we see Charlie "King Kong" Keller II. Charlie, a Frederick sport's hero, agreed to meet and said, "You have to get in the game. The money is in the Major Leagues."

He added words of wisdom that I never forgot:

Have a good attitude.
Never get on your teammates if they make an error.
Never argue with, or show up, an umpire.
Don't write bad letters when it is about your contract.
Be polite to all staff and players in the organization.

At that time, both of his boys had signed with the Yankee farm system and I'm sure he gave them the same advice. His thoughtful words would guide me throughout my baseball career.

The following evening I received a phone call from Hal Keller, Assistant Farm Director, of the newly formed expansion Washington Senators and brother of Charlie Keller, II. Hal said he wanted to talk to me and asked me not to sign with anyone until we met. Two days later, we met at my house where Mom prepared a delicious steak dinner. We joked that normally he should be treating us to dinner!

The meeting went well, and Hal offered me the same deal the Orioles were offering. It was a modest salary with a deferred bonus if I signed a Major League contract. Within days I was a Washington Senator.

Years later, while reflecting on my career, I have concluded that had I been offered a larger bonus I would've been worth more to the organization to protect, or possibly trade. As it was, they had little money invested in me.

Part Two

MY PROFESSIONAL BASEBALL CAREER WASHINGTON SENATORS ORGANIZATION – 1961 TO 1969

23

MAKING THE CUT

I was emotionally relieved and extremely optimistic about my future. I trusted I was in good hands with the Kellers looking after me.

The Washington Expansion Senators were formed after the original Washington Senators team moved to Minnesota to become the Minnesota Twins in late 1960 when eight owners approved the addition of four expansion teams. To keep a franchise in Washington D.C., the Washington Expansion Senators was formed. Existing teams selected players to build the four newly formed expansion teams. Thus, the Senators were a collection of players, coaches, and managers who were new to each other as a group.

I was off to Spring Training in Fernandina Beach, Florida, the Spring Training facility for the newly formed Pensacola Senators franchise, a new member of the Alabama Florida league, Class D Minor League baseball. For a country boy from Maryland there were a lot of firsts. It was my first jet plane ride. It was my first long bus ride from Jacksonville to Fernandina Beach. I was alone navigating new places. I checked into the Lake Wales hotel and was given an itinerary with meal times and first day workouts listed.

We had 30 to 35 guys work out as part of the Senators organization. Some of the players came from the Bluefield League in West Virginia, a rookie league composed of outstanding college and high school athletes. They were all trying to become professional baseball players. During this time a lot of faces changed as people left, new ones came, with everyone competing to make the 25 man Pensacola Senators team roster.

We used the Minnesota Twins practice field and stadium when they were out of town, but when they were in town we practiced in an unused field, which reminded me of home. It was essentially a sandlot/pasture. It didn't seem that professional, but it was better than being at home.

We ate at 6 AM. By 8 AM we were doing calisthenics, base running, pick offs and run downs. Our morning routine also included running around the field, running out to first base and being timed how fast we could cover 90 feet. We were timed running to second base, third base, and finally home, taking speed times at each base. Everyone participated including catchers, fielders and pitchers. Sometimes coaches would divide the pitchers and catchers and have some of them work out in the morning and others in the afternoon in different locations around the sandlot/pasture. All this was covered day in and day out.

When we had an intrasquad game that took place at 1 o'clock, the coaches rescheduled activities before lunch and the ball game. The intrasquad games had two or three innings so it was a pretty full day, and everyone was involved. The intense schedule broke up a number of ball players as the workouts were quite grueling.

If the Twins were in town, sometimes we studied them during their practices, with Archie Wilson, our manager, describing the action on the field. The Minnesota organization was smoother running because they were not an expansion club like our group with new players, coaches, and other staff. Plus, we were constantly rotating from the stadium to the sandlot, depending if the fields were being used.

Since I had pitched only six games, I had a lot of catching up to do. I pitched one, two, or three innings on a rotating basis with the other pitchers. I threw against the wall to improve my arm strength. A practice strategy I created to develop control was, having two men at home plate, each with a bat, and a catcher between them. I would try to throw strikes. I needed control because when we played, I either walked players with bases loaded, or I struck out the side. I was striving for consistency.

I didn't want to miss my chance to make the club. Once Spring Training had moved along and we broke camp for Pensacola, Florida, the facilities were better, and so were the results.

My first roommate was a left-handed pitcher. I never thought much about him being left-handed and how he could compromise my making the ball club. As Spring Training moved forward very quickly, I noticed his work ethic and skill were not a threat to me. Turnover was pretty common with players released from one team showing up at another camp hoping for a tryout. If a player got hurt, it gave another guy a chance to play and fill-in. The team picked some players to fill in spots. What were you going to do? Some players signed for a month. The Farm Directors had total control of all the players. Looking back, that was a very uncomfortable and threatening feeling since we did not have free agency. It would be almost 10 years later that players finally had the right to negotiate their own contracts.

Major League Shutout Debut

The last morning of Spring Training, Archie Wilson was headed for the bulletin board with the list of players who made the club. I was sitting alone in the lobby after a sleepless night, worrying about whether I had done enough to make the team. I questioned whether I pitched enough. With sunrise as a backdrop, he looked over and said "Lefty, you're going. So relax." I was so relieved, excited, and very proud that I had accomplished what I had set out to do.

24

GETTING PAID TO PLAY

Twenty-four of us successful enough to make the club with the Washington Senators were on our way to D ball Pensacola in the Alabama Florida League. These were exciting times for us! We were actually getting paid to play baseball! We were reminded regularly that getting paid to play meant we had the responsibility to act professionally and maintain decorum at all times. Fans were paying to see us, and we owed them our best effort.

As we approached the city of Pensacola, one large building stood out, the San Carlos Hotel. This hotel is where we stayed until we located our own housing. Some housing had been prearranged. It depended on where players wanted to stay, how far they from the park they wanted to be, and what transportation they needed. Most of us did not want to be too far from the ballpark because temperatures hovered around 100°F. Walking or public transportation were our only options because most of our money went toward meals. I was getting $350 per month which in today's

Major League Shutout Debut

money would be about $3600 per month. During spring training, the club picked up lodging and meals. Once the season began, we were on our own to find affordable housing and continue to eat well to maintain good health and conditioning.

As we approached the San Carlos Hotel, we were greeted with a loud round of applause. Even though it was early spring, it was extremely humid, much like Maryland and Virginia in the summer. As we exited our unairconditioned bus the crowd of about 30 fans continued cheering and waving. Yes, we felt special! We were celebrities.

We moved quickly inside due to the heat, and were met by a friendly young lady named Rosebud, who was helpful in getting us settled in the hotel. She liked matchmaking as we learned, and especially, fixing up the ball players with girls from town.

The owner of the ball club, Joe Pannicione, welcomed us. He introduced our manager, Archie Wilson. Archie had played ball in Toronto for seven seasons and, as he claimed later, he made more money in the Minors in Canada than some Major League players did in the states.

Next, we were introduced to the Hopkins Boarding House representative who extended a warm welcome to us as well. There were hors d'oeuvres circulated through the crowd and plenty of refreshing drinks for us. What the event turned out to be was an advertisement for the boarding house and the large houses adjacent to the boarding house.

Most of the guys who tried to pair up were from the Chicago area. Others knew each other from previous years. I didn't know anybody very well and ended up with a room by myself for a short time. It didn't matter who you roomed with because there were always people being released and new players coming to try out. After the first year, I roomed with Carlos "The Chief" Medrano, Bud Mattingly, and Steve Brackin.

Getting Paid to Play

Marge Smith was the administrative contact working with the Senators organization and the Pensacola Senators. She was about as close to management as we ever got. She was helpful in suggesting accommodations, restaurants and offering general helpful advice. We didn't have much personal time to figure things out due to our rigorous work schedule. In the evenings she enjoyed sitting around the lobby, singing, and having us join in. It was relaxing and something different to think about after spending a hard day with our noses to the grindstone.

The more experienced players were often out looking for a bar or a place to hang out. They also had a little bit more money to spend on socializing. Carlos and I wanted to make the club so we stayed close together most of the time. If he wanted to go someplace I would tag along or vice versa. Marge was helpful but if we had questions about the organization, she was quiet. There was not much discussion about owners or the organization in Washington. There may have been talk about who scouted us and signed us, but it was small talk and there was not much of it.

April 4 was opening night in Fort Walton Beach, as I recall. The team was bused to their ballpark with a goal to kick their butts because it was the Minnesota Twins. I think we won that game, but later, they came to Pensacola and returned the favor. It was exhilarating to have fans cheering for us. We definitely felt like celebrities, and never forgot that we were being paid to play and put forth a professional effort every time we put on a uniform. It was a hopeful time.

25

HOPKINS BOARDING HOUSE

It was tough being away from home for the first time, but the Hopkins Boarding House was definitely like home. The ball players were the first guys who had a crack at the rooms for rent. We divided up with two or three guys on the same floor. Multiples might even be sleeping in the same spacious bedroom. Most of the ball players stayed there.

We ate our breakfast in their cafeteria-style dining room. After a road trip it was very handy to wake up late and not have to venture out to have a good breakfast. Our food per diem went up to $2.50 in 1962. If we tried to eat three meals a day we had to shop around if we were on the road. Food was extremely important and we were not going to cut corners so we ate well when we could. We were on our own to plan when, what and where to eat so we would be on time for games and workouts.

It was helpful to be able to get late night snacks and take them to our rooms.

Cafeterias in the south were popular and were always reasonably priced places to eat. Any cafeteria or buffet style restaurant was fine because the food was fresh. The establishments were reputable and were not going to take a chance on having the ball players get sick. We were respected enough that we had delicious home cooking, including home baked desserts. My favorites were fried chicken, rhubarb pie and sweet tea.

26

FIRST START, FIRST SHUTOUT

My first professional start was in Pensacola pitching against the Selma Cloverleafs in 1961 in the Alabama Florida League. It had been a make-up game from a rainout the previous day.

Nine innings is what was necessary to qualify as a complete game, unless it was a doubleheader. This practice had gone through the Minor League systems. If we had a rainout, the doubleheaders had one audience who attended both games. The games were limited to seven innings. If there was a tie in the seventh inning, the teams played extra innings, as in regular baseball, until one team won. I pitched a seven inning shutout in my debut but the more memorable part of the game was the shocking way it unfolded, and it had nothing to do with my pitching.

Bud Mattingly was on the mound pitching batting practice for his first time ever. His pitch was on me before I could square up, and there it was, literally plastered on my right jaw. I had ducked toward third base to no avail. Chunks of tooth fell out and lay in the dirt in front of me. An emerging disaster.

I was scheduled to start the game and was not going to give up the opportunity. The trainers advised me to take the night off, but it was to be my first start and I wanted this chance to see what I could do. I headed for the mound after being examined and given the okay by the trainers and the dentist, who was also part owner of the franchise!

The first pitch was a line drive just off my collarbone, on my pitching arm. It stood me up to the point where I wondered WTF was going on. Was my whole career going down the drain right here and now? I focused with determination, and skillfully completed the game. The injury had occurred before the game, not during the game, so that kept me engaged. I think I shocked the Selma team, who were the league leaders. That game was a one hitter—the one off my collarbone. I felt like continuing to pitch would be a personal achievement of perseverance.

The outcome of being hit in the jaw was getting two teeth pulled the next day. A third tooth was split so a bridge was constructed by the dentist. It lasted more than 50 years with some modifications and adjustments. Later, two more teeth were pulled.

I had shut out the club that was leading the league. At the time I was throwing strikes, which was not my forte, because I was wild, and I was averaging about four walks a game in a nine inning outing. With every performance I improved, and the ultimate result was my demonstration of intestinal fortitude in pitching a game with broken teeth. That should have made anybody in Major League baseball or Minor League baseball know that I was not the normal kind of kid. I was determined and willing to work hard to succeed. Who noticed? Who cared?

First Start, First Shutout

Over two seasons with the Pensacola Senators, I posted winning records each year. I pitched 81 innings in 1961 and 162 innings in 1962.

I was the kid who signed a professional contract having only pitched six games prior to signing. My learning curve was steep and the results were motivating.

Confidence in my prospects to achieve my ultimate goal and reach the Major Leagues was high during 1961. Getting closer!

27

TEMPTATIONS

While rooming at the Hopkins Boarding House a situation occurred that was uncomfortable and difficult to navigate politely. I was approached by an attractive young lady who worked at the boarding house. She served our food as we went through the cafeteria line. She often smiled at me, and sometimes whispered to her colleague as she looked my way. One day she shyly said she was interested in me. I was surprised because I had taken her behaviors as just being friendly. I wanted to give a non-emotional answer because I didn't want to offend her, and I was flattered. But I knew what the answer had to be. I was there to work on my skills and hopefully reach the Major Leagues. I did not want to be in a situation that might jeopardize those goals.

Throughout our travels, we encountered many attractive, young ladies. There were many temptations as the locals treated us like celebrities. Women followed the players from town to town. Guys had regular dates already set up in towns on our schedule.

Major League Shutout Debut

We were often invited to private homes for dinner. It was quite a new experience to have women coming to the ballpark just to see us. The popular movies *Bull Durham* and *Major League* depict similar temptations accurately.

The more experienced guys often knew ladies in different cities whom they would visit when we were in town. They were more confident in their status on the team and were discreet and private with their after hours activities. Married players were rarely around after practices and games when we were home as their families dominated any free time. On the road, some veterans, married or single, spent free time "working the streets."

It was important to me to remember that I was there to play ball. That was my focus.

28

LAKE WALES RUMBLE

After one particular practice we headed to a nearby nightclub. Not my usual evening activity, but I happened to be with a well-known player, his girlfriend, and a female driver I did not know.

When we got to the club, we met a guy there who had been released by another club, and had shown up at our camp that morning. He hoped he might be able to hook onto one of the Minor League clubs for the year. We all had a drink together.

One lady whose husband was in Vietnam had a fondness for tequila. The local friends of her husband kept an eye on her so nobody would get out of control. She wasn't in our group, but she started to do a dirty dance on top of one of the tables. When she started taking her clothes off, the protective locals tried to pull her down from the table. A few disappointed customers protested and wanted her to keep dancing. Suddenly all hell broke loose. It was a slug fest between the locals and a few angry drunks.

I quickly headed for the exit with my group. Luckily, the four of us were not touched by any of the troublemakers who were wildly throwing punches everywhere. As we reached our car, we saw the new guy come out of the club. He was getting beaten to a pulp against a car. All at once a left hook knocked him to the ground. He slowly pulled himself up and staggered back inside.

We headed back to the hotel. Nothing happened to us and I attributed it to being with a well-known ballplayer and our quick exit. I wished that the girls we were with had known this club was rough.

We didn't know it at the time, but the new guy eventually made it back to the hotel after being roughed up quite a bit. The next day, he took batting practice, pitched, caught balls in the infield, and hit infield. During the time he was taking batting practice and catching balls he purposely walked into a bat. The bat hit him on the wrist. We found out later, once camp had broken up, that he had gone for an examination. In the hotel lobby he told us that he had broken his wrist the night before.

It was surprising what guys did. I guess he felt like the ball club might take care of him. I don't remember his name. I just remembered that he had been released and joined us that morning and the next day he had a broken wrist. How quickly baseball dreams could end.

This drama was new for a country boy from Maryland. It was like being on a movie set. Another lesson learned— Know who you are with and where you are going.

29

THANKS, JOE

I had pitched poorly that night as a long reliever. I needed to be more consistent if I was going to work my way into the starting rotation. To punish myself I decided to walk 28 blocks home alone in the dark. Usually the players walked in small groups, but tonight was different. I was beating myself up, mentally wondering what I could have done better in the game.

As I was walking along, the owner of the ball club, Joe Pannicione, drove by, recognized me, and stopped his car. He firmly reminded me that walking alone at night in this neighborhood was not advisable. He gestured for me to get in the car and gave me a ride home to the Hopkins Boarding House.

Joe was the first owner of the Peninsula Senators when they established the single A franchise in Pensacola in 1961. Joe was not only co-owner of the Peninsula Senators, but he was also a former umpire in Triple A Minor League baseball.

Major League Shutout Debut

The long walk could have had dangerous results. It was a dangerous neighborhood and players should not be out by themselves. I'll always remember Joe as a pleasant person and a hands-on owner who always looked after his players. He was the only owner I really knew until I got out of baseball.

30

PAUL RAYBON

*P*layer down! Call the trainer! Those were words we never wanted to hear, but occasionally a player was hit and we never knew how the incident would resolve itself. It was 1961 and the Pensacola Senators were playing the Selma Cloverleafs in Selma, Alabama. The two competitors had traded first place all season so the rivalry was intense.

Trainer Paul Raybon rushed out onto the field. He was always prepared with a medicine bag filled with first aid supplies. Our player, knocked down while at bat, was grabbing his arm. Paul carefully examined the arm and put a freeze spray on the injury to minimize the swelling. The crowd seemed agitated by the game delay, perhaps questioning whether the injury was really serious. There was an undercurrent of chatter that escalated. Suddenly a fan jumped out of the stands and rushed onto the field, running toward Paul and our player. The fan lunged at Paul and knocked him to the ground.

A melee ensued as both dugouts emptied with players rushing onto the field. A fight should not have occurred because the situation was about a fan, not a player, rushing our trainer. Manager Archie Wilson was all over the fan who had knocked Paul down. Wilson was an experienced manager, accustomed to breakouts, and quickly took charge. Players were rolling on the ground, hitting each other, clearly filled with frustration. Police arrived so quickly it was as though they had been in the stands. Additional squad cars arrived from outside the stadium within minutes. Police and managers corralled the players back into their respective dugouts and the game continued. The aggressive fan was subdued and removed from the stadium.

Paul and our injured player handled the situation calmly. Both were more shocked and shaken, than further injured. We learned that the fan was angered at seeing a black trainer. The racial tension in Selma was reaching a feverish pitch but this incident was a first for us. We were glad that there were no additional injuries or problems during that series and that our injured player was soon back in the lineup. Paul never expressed any reaction or anger, that I recall.

Paul was a vital member of our team. As our trainer, he was always patching up players with minor injuries or massaging sore muscles. He drove our rickety, old team bus from town to town and figured out the best places for us to stop and eat. He took care of our equipment and managed to always have our shoes polished and uniforms cleaned before the next game.

Paul joked around with us, often teasing guys whose uniforms were still clean after a game! He, himself, was meticulous in a white shirt and pants, which never seemed to get dirty. Players teased Paul, always ready to attend to an injury with his freeze bomb, and called him "Mr. Freeze." Players joked that he was the best horse trainer in organized baseball! We were in good hands with Paul.

31

LIAR LIAR

It was February and I had just received my contract in the mail. After my strong performance the previous year I anticipated a favorable contract with a decent salary increase. That is not what I saw in the mail.

I had discussed my contract with Charlie Keller, II earlier. He advised me to be polite and reasonable in a request for a salary increase. He told me not to go to Spring Training without an agreement in writing. I had played my first year of professional baseball and had broken in very well. Management knew how well I played because I had been optioned up to Triple A Syracuse for protection.

My next move was to decline the contract in writing. As much as I wanted to play ball, I was worth more than they were offering and was willing to risk my future. I called Marge in the Washington Senators Minor League office to see if she had any advice. She indicated that there had been some contract disputes with several of the guys and it might be a difficult situation to overcome with the new Assistant Farm Director. Because of the expansion franchise everyone was new. However, since I had known Hal Keller, and with him now in charge of the farm directing office, surely the assistant would be well qualified and informed. It was unsettling to hear that there were so many disputes and contracts being declined.

I followed up my letter with a phone call to the Assistant Farm Director. After hearing my concerns, he agreed to a salary increase following a brief, but cordial conversation. He urged me to get to Pensacola as soon as possible. Marge made the travel arrangements and I headed to Pensacola from my home in Maryland.

Upon arrival I headed to the Assistant Farm Director's office. There were very few happy faces coming out of his office, but I was not concerned. I was glad we had come to an agreement already. When it was finally my turn, he and I exchanged a few pleasantries, and he presented the contract. He said, "I'd like for you to sign it right away and get checked in down at the ballpark. If you can't do it today, maybe we can get it done early tomorrow morning."

I glanced over the multi-page contract to verify the numbers coincided with our phone conversation.

After a quick look, I said, "I'm sorry, but this is the same salary you mailed to me originally. Nothing has changed in the contract from our discussion about the salary increase you agreed to."

He said, "No, it's the amount you and I agreed to on the phone."

I responded, "I'm sorry, it is not what we discussed." I tried to be as polite as I could. He was obviously agitated and said tersely, "I can't have a liar in my camp. You are a liar, because that is not what we agreed on. We did not agree on an increase."

I responded, "I'm sorry, but you definitely did agree to a salary increase."

He angrily stammered, "I want you out of here" and pointed toward the door. "I want you out of my camp. Now!"

Quickly, I headed out the door where Marge was sitting at her desk. She cast a quick glance at me, and maybe wiggled her finger, but out the door I hurried, without stopping to chat.

All my belongings were at the hotel so there was no reason to stop by the ballpark. I certainly didn't want to explain what had just happened to anybody who was there. All I needed to do was check out. My next move was to grab a bite to eat and figure out how I was going to get home. My brain was racing. How could anyone use such harsh language? Had I deserved it? Had I been unreasonable? I was feeling empty and miserable. Deep down I felt I was right. I did what Charlie advised. I had earned what I asked for in my contract. If I had been worth more to the organization I could have negotiated directly with the General Manager. I wished I had talked to Marge about the possibilities for transportation home but everything transpired so quickly I never thought of it.

At the hotel there was a note from the Assistant Farm Director that read:

Don't let Don Loun leave the camp before he sees me.

Now what! It couldn't get much worse! Maybe he would accuse me of something else. I was feeling poorly and he was the last person I wanted to see, but I went back to his office.

The long lines were gone for the first time, so Marge quickly directed me into his office where he was sitting behind his desk. He motioned for me to come over and sit down in front of him. He seemed different, but I didn't know why. When he started to speak, I noticed his voice had softened and he was more at ease.

He started the conversation by saying, "I got a little hotheaded and shouldn't have, but I thought we had an agreement. I think what I did was get you confused with someone else. It's been a pretty hectic day today and here's the contract that I think we talked about."

As I took the contract from him, I could clearly see that changes had been inked in where the salary numbers had been. Sure enough, the salary increase we had verbally agreed to had been corrected. Excellent! All I had to do was sign it. I had no reason not to sign it. However, I wanted to read through it anyway. He anxiously waited while I read.

Finally, I looked up at him and said, "I can't sign this contract. I agree that it's the amount we discussed, but you called me a liar, and you told me you did not want a liar in your camp. I think that deserves an apology."

He nervously looked at me, head shaking, and quietly uttered, "I was wrong, and I apologize."

I sat silently for a moment and decided that apology was enough, and that he meant it. I signed the contract, shook hands, and got the hell out of there. As I left, Marge waved me over.

She whispered, "I want to see you in the lobby later this evening." I gestured OK and left the building.

Later that evening, she grabbed my arm, and said, "You really made me proud today. I didn't know how you would handle that situation but I'm glad you asked for an apology."

Money was one thing but an apology was something that sticks with you. It was the right thing to do even though it was not in my nature to question authority. I felt good about her kind words and told her that her comments affirmed my decision to address the situation.

It always surprised me why that fellow had been hired because a lot of the players had difficulty with him. He did not last long with the system. I wondered if the person who brought him into the organization might not have known too much about him.

Everyone was scrambling to find places to live, and we had about a month to do that before Spring Training began. I was now ready for my second year and excited to improve on the first year.

32

SELMA 1962

As we crossed the Edmund Pettus Bridge into Selma we saw a large group of folks congregating on the opposite side. Not sure what was going on, we were somewhat oblivious to the civil unrest that was happening in the south.

The Edmund Pettus Bridge was named after a former Confederate general, a US Senator, and state leader of the Ku Klux Klan. Later, it became famous forever on March 7, 1965, Bloody Sunday. It became the site of a conflict when police attacked civil rights demonstrators with tear gas and clubs as they were marching toward the state capitol.

When we arrived in town we just went straight to our hotel in Selma. We were leading in the Alabama Florida league and that was our focus. Paul Raybon, our driver and trainer, never said anything to us about his feelings regarding racial tensions. My recollection is that the subject was not discussed.

We accepted segregation in those days and did not ask questions. It was the norm. After unloading our baggage and the players, Paul drove himself to a neighborhood where he stayed overnight. He did not stay in the hotel with us. Later, he told us he ate delicious home cooking, and had been well taken care of in a comfortable, private home.

Our hotel, The Albert, was elegantly furnished and very grand. It was unfortunate that we had no cameras, and never took any videos of such a beautiful hotel. Also, we didn't have pictures of any of the unrest going on outside. The "Whites Only" signs on the restroom doors were odd to us. We did not have them in Maryland. Some of the poorly written signs read "Negroes out back" and had a painted arrow pointing outside. It all seemed so disrespectful to me.

In the hotel, we saw elegantly dressed porters. They wore silky shirts with lace collars and sleeves. Their pants were bloused below the knee and they wore white hose. Most of them were very slim, tall men who were very polite. When the porters weren't waiting on guests, they used huge feather dusters to sweep the teakwood crown molding that was along the ceiling perimeter of the lobby. The men were tall enough that they could use those dusters to reach the ceiling without ladders. It was such an elegant site. I wished we had pictures of that stately hotel.

It was surprising that surrounding us so much historical action would happen here in the future, including the march with Dr. Martin Luther King, Jr., on that very bridge we crossed. As we chugged along in our refurbished school bus, we looked out the window at how different Alabama was from Florida. Mainly, we saw shabby signs pointing to the different areas where folks were allowed, or not allowed. Similarly, it was 100° in the shade in

Selma 1962

Pensacola and we were soaking wet with perspiration. That's the way it was, without AC.

As I think back on our series in Selma, I don't recall any disturbances that caused events to be canceled while we were in town. I remember that we ate lunch at the counter at a Walgreens in Selma. Only two years earlier, in 1960, there had been a sit-in at another Walgreens lunch counter.

Selma had a great team and we traded first place all season. In this outing we swept the series. We were excited about clinching first place and the pennant for the year. We clinched it earlier than any team ever had, and had the best win-loss percentage (.710) in professional baseball history, as I recall. It was August 2, 1962. We did it with four left-handed starters. We carried that pride through our time in professional baseball.

33

OZARK

Ozark, Alabama, was about 150 miles from Pensacola, Florida. We were on a one day road trip to a place we hadn't been before in our rickety, steamy, black school bus. With poorly marked rural roads, we had gotten lost trying to locate the substitute ballpark. Paul Raybon knew the back roads pretty well, but in this case, it seemed our main road to the game was inaccessibile.Their ballpark was being used for the annual carnival that was in town!

After traveling most of the day we finally arrived at the makeshift elementary school ballpark at game time! No real dugout. No real stadium. No time to eat. No hotel tonight because we planned to head back after the game. We had already changed into our uniforms on the bus amid all the equipment and sweltering heat. It couldn't have gotten much worse unless it had rained with thunder, lightning and flooding!

I was the starting pitcher. I started the ball game with little time to loosen up and execute my usual warm-up routine.

However, I focused and soon had command of my rhythm. I finished the ball game having pitched a complete game and shut the team out.

After the game, we ate hotdogs and other leftover food from the food truck. It was surprising how friendly our hosts were considering we had just kicked their butts. With no time for showers, we changed shirts, hustled to the bus, and headed back to Pensacola, where we arrived about 2 AM.

In the Minor Leagues you never know what you might learn about yourself. This trip was an education for me. What I learned was that it didn't matter what normal routine I was accustomed to before the ball game. I had assumed my usual routine was essential to my success. It was not the key. My overall preparedness gave me the confidence to overcome an unusual situation. You never know where your confidence comes from and how you build on it. Just go out there and get the job done.

34

FRED WATERS

Fred Waters was one of the best pitching coaches I ever had. He had enjoyed a successful career with the Pittsburgh Pirates. After professional baseball, he became a high school baseball coach and a coach-pitcher for Pensacola. My roommate, Carlos, and I, agreed that we learned more from Fred Waters than any other coach. He taught me how set up hitters, take notes on hitters and how fast they ran, and what pitch you got them out with. Watching another lefty throw and workout taught me a lot about pitching. Most of all, he took a personal interest in all the pitchers. In fact, he was the saving grace for most of the pitchers. Some of them had gotten pretty good money to sign and his help was beneficial. I was not a "bonus baby."

Fred told me he could not understand why I had not pitched on a regular basis during my first year, 1961. He had heard rumors that I was credible, and was in demand by other clubs, even though I only had a 5-3 record and about 12 starts. I had a lack of control, but was strong. He thought I needed more work, not less. After all, I had only pitched six games prior to signing, so it was clear I had mechanical problems. However, I remedied issues as quickly as I could with Fred's direction.

By the 1962 season, I was one of the most improved pitchers. I had compiled a 9-5 record until I joined the Army Reserves and missed a complete rotation. I missed two starts and lost control with the baseball because I didn't hold it or do anything with it for two weeks. Gradually, I lost up to nine games, including three consecutive losses.

I finished the season at 11-9. I had a better record than the stats showed. I was developing a modest pick off move, great slider, and a straight change "lampshade." I was protected on the Triple A roster seven out of nine years.

35

YOU DON'T DECIDE YOUR FUTURE

You don't decide your future. (a rant based on conversations with experienced players and scouts)

It only took a little over a year for me to begin to notice that my future was largely not in my hands.

Older players often told us that the organization had the ability to make judgments that influenced a player's success and progress, or prohibited movement. An evaluation was not always conducted by someone qualified to do it. The interpretation of a player's performance was highly subjective.

Who was paying attention to you as an individual player? Were there notes, reports, conversations and discussions that took place that could affect a player's progress that the player himself was privy to, or allowed input? Personal issues such as health, marriage status, personality, attitude and family connections could be factors influencing a player's ability to succeed.

Major League Shutout Debut

Who was making the decisions about your future? Coaches, owners, managers, YES! Also, their buddies and former teammates. It may have been baseball knowledge that propelled staff upward with the organization, but decision making did not necessarily reflect good judgment. Was an evaluation based on the players ability or an opinion by the evaluator?

I never felt confident once I learned that was the process and heard the comments made by scouts and older players about guys who had been in the game. That did not seem a fair way to judge a player. It also meant hard work may not pay off. Performance should count.

Decision makers were often transient. Since they may leave the organization at any time, there was no long-term reason to actually care about an individual player or be loyal to the organization.

Biased newspaper reporting could influence the progress of baseball players with negative reports. Some players were not flamboyant, but had talent, weren't glittery and full of diamonds, but were down to earth, and were overlooked.

In the 1960s the trend was moving away from the gut busting guys who played the game and knew the game. There were some players who were learning the game but never got an opportunity to advance. Who a player was signed by could play a part in that player's opportunities. The future was cut off when players were in Triple A or maybe even Double A. They may have been making good money because of a contract that they agreed to, or because of some success they may have had. They may have held out for a contract that was built on the future. That could happen to scouts or coaches, also. It was probably played on because there wasn't the big money in baseball that there is today, but it was good money for work that was being done.

Sometimes a seed is planted and you want it to grow. It grows and the next thing you know it blooms. It did exactly what you hoped it would do. But that flower may not be as attractive to the decision makers as another flower, so one is overlooked.

Perhaps the organization builds a good contract because the management sees that a player has capabilities but it never comes to fruition. Tradable players were being used in a way that they would not know. They may be allowed to perform on a regular basis or they could possibly be held back for reasons that the organization deemed necessary but would never tell the player.

Bottom line. Evaluation was often based on subjective judgment and money rather than performance.

36

DUTY CALLS

Hal Keller arranged for me to join the Army Reserves. The timing was arranged at Keller's request and Uncle Sam's approval to protect my future in baseball and get my service commitment fulfilled right away. I was playing well and showing a lot of potential in the spring of 1962. I didn't know when I would be called.

When the season ended I phoned home to announce that I had an offer to play in Nicaragua for the winter. My mother informed me that a letter had arrived, and the Army had a different plan for me. I was excited to fulfill my military obligation, but I was disappointed to skip Winter Ball. Washington decided to have their own team and I wanted to keep working on my game. But I had to miss it.

I headed to basic training in Fort Knox, Kentucky in late August. One thing I did not want to do during the winter months was wash out. It was a rough winter and we were put through a lot of drills. The military does not cut back, but at one point it seemed they let up a little bit because we could defend our reserve unit, whether it was in the states or, if we were shipped out. Usually guys who went into the service in August, as I did, ended up doing the Santa Claus plan, and got out for Christmas. I finished up in March.

I served eight years in the Army Reserves. No complaints. I know was one of the lucky ones during the turbulent 1960s. I fulfilled my obligation and was proud to do so.

37

BEST RECORD

It was August: hot, humid, bugs, typical Florida in August. Our Pensacola team had already clinched the "pennant." I was not there when they actually clinched and I never saw a physical "pennant." I had just returned from joining the Army in my hometown. I had already committed what turned out to be a cardinal sin by not having a baseball constantly in my pitching hand. I did not have a baseball the whole six months I was in basic training. I wasn't thinking about the game. Big mistake!

My 9 and 5 record and ERA below three went in the toilet and I was off to a slow restart for what limited experience I had at that time. I struggled through the next five starts. Getting back in the groove took too long. Ending the season with a record of 11 wins and 9 losses was a real setback for me because I had been on a roll before enlisting. A lot of those ball games would not have been losses had I been advised to keep the baseball in my hand to maintain "feel." This was a costly lesson to have learned.

Major League Shutout Debut

That's what the Minor Leagues were all about; learn something new every day. It was definitely a training ground for the Major Leagues. This was a great year for the ball club as baseball had returned to Pensacola the past 2 years because of the Senators organization. 1961 was extremely experimental, but in 1962 we ran away with the pennant. It was a learning curve for all involved from top to bottom.

After clinching the pennant in early August, the team became complacent, and lost focus temporarily when players were sent down from the rookie league to see what they could do. It threw our rotation out of sync for a while, but we finished up strong. We took first place in the Alabama Florida League with a 79-38 record and had the only winning record in the league. Fort Walton finished second with a 58-61 record. The most noteworthy memory is that we used five left-handed starters, which was quite unusual, and still is unusual. But it worked. I recall Fred Waters, Bob Baird, Carl Middledorf, Doug Ritter and myself as the left-handed starting pitchers in rotation.

When the season ended there was no place to go except South America and play Winter Ball. That's where we, as prospects, would end up, from the first of September, or as late as the first of October. The manager of this ball club was a little bit short on educating himself about his pitching staff. Had he had more knowledge it may have made a difference in two or three ball games. Fred Waters was the stand-in, assumed pitching coach. He was never recognized for that position but should have been. That way, I think all the staff would have excelled except for a couple of guys. Some players just never made it out of D-ball, or later, as Class A.

The Minor Leagues were getting rid of D, C, and B classifications and everything was coming under A. That meant fewer jobs for all of us, including coaches, players, and management. I felt strongly about getting talent from the rookie league. The rookie league was jam-packed with players, but not necessarily future prospects. They were guys coming out of college and had a little more experience than most of the guys we had in 1961.

Fundamentally, we were very sound and made the plays. Very seldom did you throw to the wrong base or set up the wrong defense for hitters. It was a real test for our pitchers to be able to control the baseball and that matured as the year passed.

My roommate spent 11 years in the Minor Leagues and that was a failing of the organization, in my opinion. Somewhere, somehow, he should have gotten a shot, maybe even a pension. Something in the organization wanted to dump us all. I think the lack of interest in us was noticeable as we were ignored, undervalued, and under promoted. The Boston Red Sox saved one of the players, John Kennedy, because they worked him in a trade. His familiar name may have been helpful. I never knew if, or when, we were being looked at as trade bait.

The 1960s were a transition time. Very few good, experienced hitting and pitching instructors who knew fundamentals were available. Plus, owners were cheap and didn't want to pay a guy with a family who previously had a Big League career or had been in the Minor Leagues where he made more money.

Ending the 1962 season with a 11-9 record was personally disappointing. I felt Winter Ball was needed to help me develop consistency and work on my pitches and general game. I was still protected and they gave me a small salary increase so the end of the season was mildly successful. Looking back, trading me would have been a good move for the organization, and especially, for me.

38

TURNING POINT

The Carolina League was the turning point of my career.
I was promoted to the Class A Carolina League in March 1963. We headed for Peninsula, which had been the home of the Peninsula Grays in the Hampton Newport News, Virginia area. This ball club was just barely good enough to win ball games, but it seemed that they won when I was in the game.

Rumor had it a Dodger affiliate named Koufax had shown up for a refresher before going on with his career. Sandy almost quit baseball before that last year. My understanding was that Doug Camilli was the man who made Sandy Koufax take a hard look at himself, and the rest is history.

I started out well, which seemed to be my usual beginning. If it wasn't a shutout, it was close, because I threw five shutouts during this year.

A guy by the name of Lou Piniella came out of the Indian organization and joined our club after a big trade. Lou was included

Major League Shutout Debut

as a Minor League player and joined us in the Carolina League with the newly named Peninsula Senators. Lou and Brant Alyea became good buddies. I used to call them Pete and Repeat. Lou became frustrated when he did not play well. He took out his frustrations on Paul Raybon's medicine bag by pounding on it every time he struck out or made an out. He didn't think anybody should get him out, so he led the league in destroying medicine bags. Archie Wilson, our manager, had Lou replace all of the medicine bags he destroyed. He was the uncontested leader in breaking up medicine bags and replacing them.

Lou made one of the best catches I ever saw while playing centerfield. He ran straight towards our scoreboard in left field and made a barehanded diving catch into a gravel pit. It was the best one I ever saw. Most guys couldn't catch the ball with a glove hand. He was right-handed and just grabbed the ball with his bare hand or he wouldn't have caught it at all. It was such an outstanding catch you had to be there to appreciate it. The crowd went wild.

On my own search for stardom I found out that records usually accompanied low hit ball games. I had a no-hitter going in 8 2/3 innings in a well attended Pony Day game. Jim Martin, first baseman, was closest to the ball. The batter hit a ground ball to first base. I covered for the out. That was about the third or fourth inning. In the ninth inning a ball was hit in the gap between second and first. Jim Martin didn't dive for it. What! Not what I would have expected. The ball was not coming. Jim ran over and told me that he didn't want everyone to call him a hot dog if he had to dive after the ball. He said he thought he could have gotten it. I basically turned my back because we were done. That was a play we practiced constantly and he didn't even attempt it. It wasn't something you wanted to hear. If you've toiled for 8 2/3 innings and had the no hitter locked up, you had to face one or two more batters and the game would be on ice. Anyway, it was on ice. It was a shutout. That Pony Day happened to have over 3000 fans in attendance. It was disappointing because it was less than 100% effort and performance. I had pitched close to 500 innings so far in my career plus about 150 innings during Winter Ball.

In the Carolina League I had cut walks down to about four a game. When I played, walks were a very important part of the game and I did not want them to get out of control. But as I reflect, I realize a walk can only hurt you if it scores. So, with my shutout reputation and performances, it didn't matter if there were seven hits and I walked seven, or threw a no hitter. The walk only counts if it crosses the plate or if it forces a run to score. A pitcher can win a ball game by walking six or seven guys, and not give up any runs. In a shutout, therefore, no harm, no foul. Why should those walks not be identified in a manner that sets them up more positively from the normal walk total? Intentional walks are set up. That certainly shouldn't enter into a walk total. There were fewer walks in the Minor Leagues as a pitcher learned his trade.

Once a pitcher reaches stature in his career no one wants to see too many walks. There are times when it's better to give up the batter because when they have an intentional walk there is a suspicion you have. The odds are better for the pitcher. If the pitcher walks a player and someone is on second base and first base is open, the pitcher can intentionally walk the batter, which I applaud. Walking the batter was never an option for the pitcher to determine as a strategic move. The manager always made the call to walk a batter. It was all part of the learning curve.

The season was win, lose, lose, win, lose, lose, win, win. The ball club was just not functioning well. Defensively, we were average. Hitting with men in scoring positions was awful. We didn't score many runs, and, if we gave up three runs, our ball club would not be in the game. Washington had a reputation that we weren't going to score many runs. So we had to play good defense. We had to knock the ball down and throw the runner out at the plate if we had any chance at all. That's the way I looked at things.

As a pitcher, my thought was to go out and shut the players down. I pitched ahead to get on the top of the hitter, stay on top of the hitter, get him out, and throw strikes. Those strategies worked to my benefit. Catching was a weak spot. We were not going to get out of a ball game without a pass ball or a wild pitch. Most of the time the error went against the pitcher because the players were either going to block the ball, or not.

There wasn't a time that I walked out on the mound that I didn't expect to finish the game. I believed that the pitcher's job was to keep the team in the game. Sometimes managers and players did not see eye to eye. If a manager wanted to go with a better situation because of the hitter, Carlos "The Chief" Medrano, relief pitcher, could get them out. The pitchers went along with that. The goal was to keep the opposition off the base.

As long as there was someone on base, the team could lose the ball game. In home game situations there was a chance to get the game back if the opposing team went ahead. We would lose in late innings if we were behind. Most of the time, in my case, it tied the game up. You have to be in it to win it. I was not happy coming out of the game, win or lose.

During that season, I started to get a little bit of a pick off move, better balance, and a better feel. All my mechanics were consistently being worked on for every game. There were certain routines I went through, having only thrown six games as an amateur. It was a constant learning situation for me and I fed off everybody. I watched the players who had good moves, and I watched how pitchers threw strikes, both right-handed and left-handed. It worked out to my benefit and helped me get through the year. This was a turning point because my pitching mechanics were coming together. I was developing a solid repertoire of pitches and my control was good.

The final game of the year for me in 1963 with the Peninsula Senators was memorable, because we came from behind and won the game. Frank Caradonna hit a drive to score the winning run. I pitched all nine innings and was the pitcher of record, and so proud. I was pleased with how many games I finished.

At the end of the season, we celebrated with a party at the house that five of us guys rented in Hampton-Newport News. What a party! People flocked in and out all evening.

After that season I moved up to AA York in 1964.

What a year in 1963! There were no awards, but plenty of rewards.

39

UNWRITTEN RULE

*A*s a pitcher you have certain responsibilities. One revolves around how an inexperienced pitcher handles an inevitable situation. If one of your players is hurt by the opposing team, it's almost impossible to understand what may take place next, because, whether it was accidental or intentional, there's a difference in how the event is handled. There may be anger. A serious injury can affect your pennant drive. How the pitcher handles the situation, especially if it's his first encounter, may reveal the kind of individual he is. Each organization covers how to deal with unique, sensitive situations its own way.

A series of events may occur. You, the pitcher, analyze the situation knowing full well that you must protect your players. The strength of a successful team is power up the middle of the diamond. The shortstop and second baseman are vital and vulnerable. Once it's understood how the situation occurred and how serious the injury, there is some justification for the pitcher the next time he faces the same player. If the injured teammate can walk off the field, a lot of jawing goes back and forth between dugouts. Everyone reacts and charges onto the field. If it was unintentional, there should not be a serious brawl, but there could be a series of retaliations. One retaliation could be dusting off the guy who hurt your player the next time he is at bat because he's responsible for being out of control.

If the teammate is going to be out of commission indefinitely the pitcher still has to take care of the problem. The umpires take control first, and warn both dugouts, and then advise the managers of each team of follow up actions. The manager will signal or tell the pitcher what he needs to do to resolve the problem.

It is an adjustment for the inexperienced pitcher because all he has been trying to do is throw strikes, control the baseball, and NOT hit the batter. Now the pitcher is faced with being asked to intentionally hit the batter.

It happened to me and my responsibility was to drill the guy during his next at bat. I had to get it done. That was a really hard adjustment for me to make because I had never had to do that before. Once I saw how he spiked my shortstop, it made it a little easier even though he pleaded he didn't do it on purpose. That doesn't matter. You have to be under control. You have to be able to take a knock down and move on.

In some cases, with the pitcher, he has to take a runner down because he was careless. For instance, if he slid into second base with spikes up trying to break up a double play, it puts the shortstop on the disabled list. If it's coming from the second baseman in line, he'll try to dance behind the base. If he is fast enough he may be able to cut in front or leap in the air. Those are the only choices he has because he's in a vulnerable position. Class A ball puts inexperienced players on the field but they have to know how to handle the situations.

Although their shortstop had played a lot of ball, he was from South America where some aspects of baseball are different. That particularly showed up in my situation. The manager has to take the responsibility. He doesn't have to say a word on the field but he will look down the bench and make sure you, the pitcher, saw it and know what to do next time you face that player.

The manager may write his reaction to the action you took. I had to knock the guy down and make him respect our club and be more in control of what he does on the ball field. If he wants to play rough, tough tag, then we can accommodate him.

I knocked their shortstop down. If the ball club substituted somebody for that player because they did not want to create an incident, you, the pitcher, don't put it off. It's not something you put off unless it's a mean situation. You take care of it during that game. If I were taken out of the game before the guy came up to bat again, or if they substituted their player, the next pitcher takes my responsibility and has to straighten out the situation.

Since the manager sets the rules, the players just act according to the plan. In my case, the retaliation could have been prevented by the opposing manager because he didn't tell a foreign player what the rules are in American baseball.

If the teams were in a playoff situation; a do or die, win or lose, or go home situation, it would be handled differently. If the new shortstop was substituted and you knocked down the substitute shortstop, the pitcher doesn't waste time waiting for the go-around. In that case you take care of it immediately. That's the only exception where you would throw at a new shortstop.

You could assume they took the other player out because he was ticked off about being bailed out, or whatever the manager decided to discuss with him that he may, or may not, have liked.

That's up to the manager. If a pitcher drills the new shortstop, that's his hard luck. It's a vicious game.

Every time you put on a uniform you're playing for money, your future, and you're being judged by people in the stands. There are people on the other club that may be traded to your club someday. Many times players already know the guys on the other team because they played with them in other organizations. Bad mouthing affects your movement in the organization and you can't risk that. You have to keep a great attitude about where you are and what you are trying to achieve. Managers manage and players play.

40

FIRST TRIPLE A SPRING TRAINING

*1*963 had been a hell of a good year for me. I should have gotten a call to join the big club at the end of the season. I was a work in progress who was developing an effective game and was successful. I was sent to Winter Ball and then up to Triple A Spring Training in Daytona Beach with rookie manager, Sparky Anderson, who was part of the Toronto Maple Leafs organization.

Sparky Anderson was new to me, but not new to baseball, as he was touted as a very capable and responsible player-manager. Players were coming from many other Major League clubs. Carlos, my roommate and teammate, and I, were the only two players selected to move up with protection on the Triple A roster over the winter of 1963. Selections of other players were made by Sparky and his right hand man, Ozzie Virgil, third base coach. I was not familiar with him, but he was in charge of players and the coaching staff. He and Sparky ran a well-organized Spring Training.

Spring Training was hard work and productive. The coaching staff had put a lot of time and effort into evaluating ball players during the workouts. Pitchers were especially schooled on how to deal with the ever-changing wind gusts in the Daytona Beach area. Cuts were made, and players were sent in other directions. Eventually, Carlos and I were sent back to the Washington organization where we joined the Double A Eastern League York White Roses in Fernandina Beach, with Manager Jim Lemon.

41

WHY NOT THE BIG LEAGUES?

*Y*ork, PA was quite wet most of the time in early spring. We had four ball games to open up the Double A Eastern League and the first two were rained out. The ballpark got a little tacky, but maintenance did a good job cleaning it. Fires were set to burn the puddles in order to dry the field. We finally played a doubleheader: one attendance split, with seven innings for each game. Attendance was generally poor due to the horrible weather.

My debut with the York White Roses turned out well with a five hit 15 strikeout win against Charleston. In my first five starts, I was 4 and 1, leading the league in ERAs and strikeouts. I was winning ball games and wasn't giving up anything except a run here and there.

Tendinitis developed in my left shoulder. I had to report to Washington where Dr. George Resta gave me a couple of shots of

Major League Shutout Debut

Cortizone and sent me back to York. Walking into Dr. Resta's office in the ballpark of the Washington Senators felt good. I wished I could have stayed with the Big Club, but I went back to York for rehabilitation. The injection had reached all of the inflamed area of my front left shoulder. All I had to do was work the soreness out like a deep bruise and break up the discoloration.

In a short period of time I was pitching again. My attitude was, "If you give me the ball, I'll play." Unfortunately, that was never written in my records that I know. What was written when I was pitching in Double A and moved up the rosters was probably that I had suffered mild tendonitis in the front left shoulder. I felt like that injury, and whatever was written about me, followed me through my career, and was likely negative. I'm not sure anything was written about my work ethic, progress or quick recovery from injury.

My first outing after rehab was a little rocky, and I gave up more than I wanted to, but when you come back from an injury having pitched only on the sidelines in batting practice, it required some adjustments. I was working all around the area because of the injection and probable scar tissue. The doctor wasn't worried about the injury. He wanted me to get well and start pitching again.

Of my 14 starts, I had 6 wins with a 2.54 ERA. I allowed 79 hits in 92 innings, averaging a strikeout every inning. My season was going well. I was ready to move up.

42

THE FINE

Our bus got in late in the afternoon to Williamsport, Pennsylvania, in the Eastern League. Jim Lemon, our manager, informed us we needed to be in the lobby at 4:00 PM, ready to go to the ballpark.

My roommate, Dalton Renfro, and I, thought we would catch a few winks before meeting the bus and we did. We reached the lobby ten minutes before the bus was scheduled to leave. No one was there. The lobby was empty. Where was everyone? The desk clerk said the bus had left a few minutes earlier. We glanced at our watches which indicated it was not yet 4:00 pm. The bus had left without us.

Fro and I took a cab to the ballpark, which we could ill afford. The judgment had been made. I never took issue with managers when they said things, but I feel that there had been a huge mistake. A fine of $25 plus cab fare had to be paid.

I scraped together what I had, including pennies, nickels, dimes, other change, and a few bills. I presented a bag of money to

Major League Shutout Debut

Jim Lemon. He appeared surprised that I would do such a thing. So was I. I don't know what drove me to pay the fine in mostly small change other than I knew I was right. I had never missed a bus. In fact, I had been early for most games and practices. The bus had left early. I paid my fine.

43

NATIONAL BASEBALL HALL OF FAME

Off to Cooperstown and the National Baseball Hall of Fame! I was awarded the opportunity to pitch in the Hall of Fame game held on July 27, 1964. It was Induction Day for the new class of Hall of Famers. As I recall, my Frederick, Maryland hometown newspaper ran a headline story on the sports page ahead of my going to Cooperstown. I was excited and assumed I was being sent there because I had been pitching so well. I did not have any input into the decision, and unfortunately, was going to miss the All-Star Eastern League Classic. I enjoyed the success I was having in York and preferred to stay there because it seemed like a better pathway to the Major Leagues. I took the bus to Cooperstown from Pittsburgh. I pitched against Casey Stengel and the Major League New York Mets.

Major League Shutout Debut

In retrospect, I have wondered how I could have qualified to pitch against a Major League team if I was a Double A pitcher. I felt like I should have been signed or moved up to Major League status. I pitched very well in the game but I think I could have done better had there not been a short porch, about 230 feet, in right centerfield.

Ultimately, I was proud to have been selected to represent York, PA, and the Senators organization. I pitched well with two out of three shutout innings.

Back in York, I continued pitching successfully. Rumors had it that I was a shoe-in for All-Star selection in the Eastern League. Unfortunately, I would not be selected because I was optioned out to Triple A Toronto about a week later.

Years later, I visited Cooperstown again with my wife and daughter. Seeing Doubleday Field brought back memories of the day I pitched in the Hall of Fame game. The family perused archived photographs from that special day. A trip worth taking.

National Baseball Hall of Fame

Visiting Doubleday Field and the National Baseball Hall of Fame with my family, 2002.

44

THE CHIEF

Even in Springfield, Massachusetts, it was a hot and humid midsummer. We had played ten consecutive days, including July 4, and needed a break. We teased The Chief Medrano about doing a rain dance because we needed a day off and we were pretty sure the people in Springfield needed some relief from the miserable heat.

The mere power of suggestion was successful, because after our victorious night game, The Chief went to the roof of the hotel, climbed on top of the generator, and started his rain dance. He was joined by a couple of players who admired how serious he was. You just couldn't stop him whooping, chanting, banging, and parading all around the rooftop. He wore a makeshift headdress that was fashioned for him from hotel supplies. A loincloth made of towels was draped around his waist. Bare-chested, The Chief looked splendid. He danced vigorously, nonstop, trying to bring on the rain!

Major League Shutout Debut

Although I was in Cooperstown, I heard about The Chief's exhibition results when the following morning fresh, cool rain poured down in buckets. Thanks to The Chief, everyone was thrilled. The game wasn't a rainout, but there was a delay because there was so much mud around the park. They had enough time to recuperate at the hotel until our 7 PM game. The rain cooled the air and fans were grateful. Everyone credited The Chief Medrano and said he would go down in infamy as The Chief of the Rain Dance in Springfield, Massachusetts.

45

WHO IS ASLEEP AT THE WHEEL?

The worst outing I had in York was in early August when I didn't have good stuff and was struggling. Jim Lemon told me he would not have left me in the game normally, but I was being sent to Triple A Toronto Maple Leafs that evening. A bad outing but a good result! Sparky Anderson needed help up there to get them in the playoffs, and I needed to leave York that very night for Toronto and the International League.

When I arrived in Toronto, they were ready to leave for a road trip to Richmond. It made me wonder who was talking to whom since I had just been in York and could have gone directly to Richmond and met the team there. Is someone asleep?

Sparky asked me where I had been, and I said, "I've been traveling."

He added, "It took you a long time to get here."

I wanted to reply, "I took a buckboard and that took a little bit longer on some pretty rough roads."

That would have been a smartass response which was not my usual style. Ever. My actual response has been forgotten.

I started the game against the New York Yankees Triple A Richmond ace, Mel Stottlemyre, on August 4. There was quite a crowd because Stottlemyre was getting a lot of press at the time. Ralph Hauk, Yankees GM, was also in attendance. A battle of shutouts between the two pitchers entertained a packed stadium until Stottlemyre was relieved after nine shutout innings. I continued pitching and shut them out for 11 2/3 innings before I was pulled by Sparky. I had a shutout going and did not want to be pulled, but I was not the manager. I had about 15 pop-ups; my straight change up and slider were working very well, and I had zero walks. A Yankee player was on second base when I was relieved. He scored, and we lost 1 to 0. I personally counted it as a shutout for at least nine innings even though that would not be classified as such in my stats. Even though I didn't give up any runs, I got charged with the loss. That's baseball.

I started eight games with Toronto, pitched in relief for one game, and came off with a 4 and 3 record with a 1.47 ERA in 55 innings. I wasn't giving up much. I hadn't pitched in the International League long enough to qualify for seasonal awards or All Star games. I was optioned so often to different clubs that I was never anywhere long enough to compile a lengthy résumé. There were other years I should have received recognition, but never did.

46

WELCOME TO THE SHOW

When we failed to make the playoffs in Toronto, Ken Retzer, my catcher, and I, went on to Detroit and met the big club. When I arrived, Claude Osteen had just beaten Detroit, 3 to 1, with 98 pitches. General Manager Selkirk smirked as he asked me if I could pitch as well as Osteen. I thought to myself, "That's why I'm here. He doesn't know what I've done to get here or he would never have asked me that question."

I answered, "I will give it my best shot." And I did. I signed a Major League contract and finished up the year as a Washington Senator.

1964 had been an amazing year. I had started Spring Training with the Peninsula Senators in the Class A Carolina League. In April I was promoted to Double A York in the Eastern League. In August I was promoted to Triple A Toronto in the International

Major League Shutout Debut

League. Five weeks later, I was promoted to the Major Leagues! From Class A to the Majors in one season!

My Major League introduction was not very smooth because I didn't get to pitch for at least 10 days because of unwritten rules about first division playoffs. The American League and the National League didn't want rookies pitching against teams that occupied the top four positions. I didn't understand why they wouldn't pitch me. My concentration level was high, they were paying me to pitch, and crowd noise never bothered me. I felt like I had to get a job done, and the way I practiced I thought I deserved a chance to perform. I was fundamentally sound. My success in the International League had given Toronto an excellent chance to make the playoffs.

On to Cleveland where Claude Osteen became my roommate. I'll always remember the hotel was packed with excited fans outside. Beatles fans! When we looked out the hotel window we saw shrieking fans looking up at us. Claude put on a black sweater, partially covering his head, and waved out the window. The noise was deafening as fans waved, blew kisses, and cheered, thinking we were the Beatles.

I did not pitch in Cleveland, but was in the bullpen, and could have pitched. We headed to DC, where Gil Hodges, the Senators manager, asked me if I could throw batting practice. Of course I could. I wasn't sure I was off to a great start with him with that kind of question being drilled at me without taking a breath: "Can you pitch 30 minutes, 20 minutes, 15 minutes, 10 minutes, 5 minutes?"

No chance to respond. Whoa!

I would not pitch until we got back to DC. The layoff did not do me any good. I was not in a regular rotation. It seemed like they were going to throw me in when it worked for them and I felt like they were going to leave me out in the cold until the last minute. I figured it would go something like this, "Lefty, you're going down to the bullpen to warm up. You're starting tonight." I was ready for that.

I kept thinking to myself, "Why won't they start me? I've earned it. I did everything a manager could want a pitcher to do."

47

MAJOR LEAGUE SHUTOUT

My first start in the Major Leagues was on September 23, 1964 against the formidable Boston Red Sox. I had been under contract but had not pitched since August except for batting practice in DC stadium. I felt rested. I was pitching by the dugout where someone had placed a pitcher's mound in front. I warmed up. The distance was fine. My routine as a starter was to throw 75 pitches.

The Star-Spangled Banner played and the game started. My catcher, Ken Retzer, and I should have met ahead of time to discuss how to pitch to their lineup. Instead, we decided I should throw strikes. The first batter for Boston was Felix Mantilla, second baseman. He led off with a double in left center. Tony Conigliaro hit a pop-up to third. I knew at that point that I needed to strike somebody out. The third batter in their lineup was Carl

Major League Shutout Debut

Yastrzemski, a left-handed hitter. I struck Carl out for the second out. That was the strikeout I needed. Dick Stuart hit a pop-up to third and the inning was over.

That's the way the game was played. Strike out people who were in scoring positions or make them hit your pitch. This strategy was not new to me, but people seem to think it was unusual for a rookie to understand. That's the way you get people out of innings.

In the third inning I remember that Tony Conigliaro came up and got a base hit. A ground ball, double play ball, was hit to Don Blasingame at second, who fielded the ball and threw it to shortstop Eddie Brinkman. As Brinkman relayed the ball to first baseman Joe Cunningham, Tony was standing up in the baseline. Brinkman hit him in the head, knocked him down, and he was out cold. It looked like Tony had his own plans to take out Brinkman, but it worked in reverse. Everybody was worried about what happened, but we had two outs.

The medics got Tony off the field.

When he came to, he said, "Where is the guy? Where is the guy?"

Eddie answered, "I'm right here if you want me. Here I am," as they carted Tony to the dugout. The next guy made the third out.

Washington's Chuck Hinton hit and got on third base and scored on a double play ball hit by Ken Retzer. That was the first two outs of the 3rd inning and that was all the scoring that happened.

In the seventh inning Frank Malzone hit a double into left center leading off the seventh inning. I caught a pop up, or ground ball. The third baseman checked him at second if it wasn't something he was going to advance on. For the next play I was contemplating strikeout as you would normally do regardless of who the batter was. I believe it was Frank Thomas who ended up taking a third called strike without questioning the pitch at all. That surprised me that he took it but we got out of the inning.

The ninth inning was the end of it. 5 hits, 0 walks, 2 strikeouts, 1-0 win, and 92 pitches later. Game over. No Red Sox player got past second base. I wouldn't pitch again until October 3 in Boston.

Another 10 days rest late in the season can work against you. Management sat on me. Why? Why didn't I fit into the rotation?

There were 1491 in attendance with about 500 from Frederick. There was very little publicity outside of Frederick before the game that mentioned a local boy trying to make his Major League debut 40 miles up the road. How about a local boy who was not a pitcher for his high school baseball team, who becomes a pitcher in the Major Leagues? That's the way things happened throughout my career.

My hometown sports writer and a writer from The Washington Post asked me after the game how I felt. I was proud but I didn't feel different than I felt with the other shutouts that I had thrown in 1963 and 1964. It wasn't that different. If you have a job to do, you gotta do it, and you go with whatever takes place.

As we left the field, Don Blasingame, second baseman, complimented me and gave me the game ball. He predicted I would be around for a long time. He also said that he would get the ball painted to commemorate this game. I still have that intricately painted keepsake from the game. Other teammates patted me on the back and shook hands. It wasn't like today's game with the water cooler being dumped and guys jumping around.

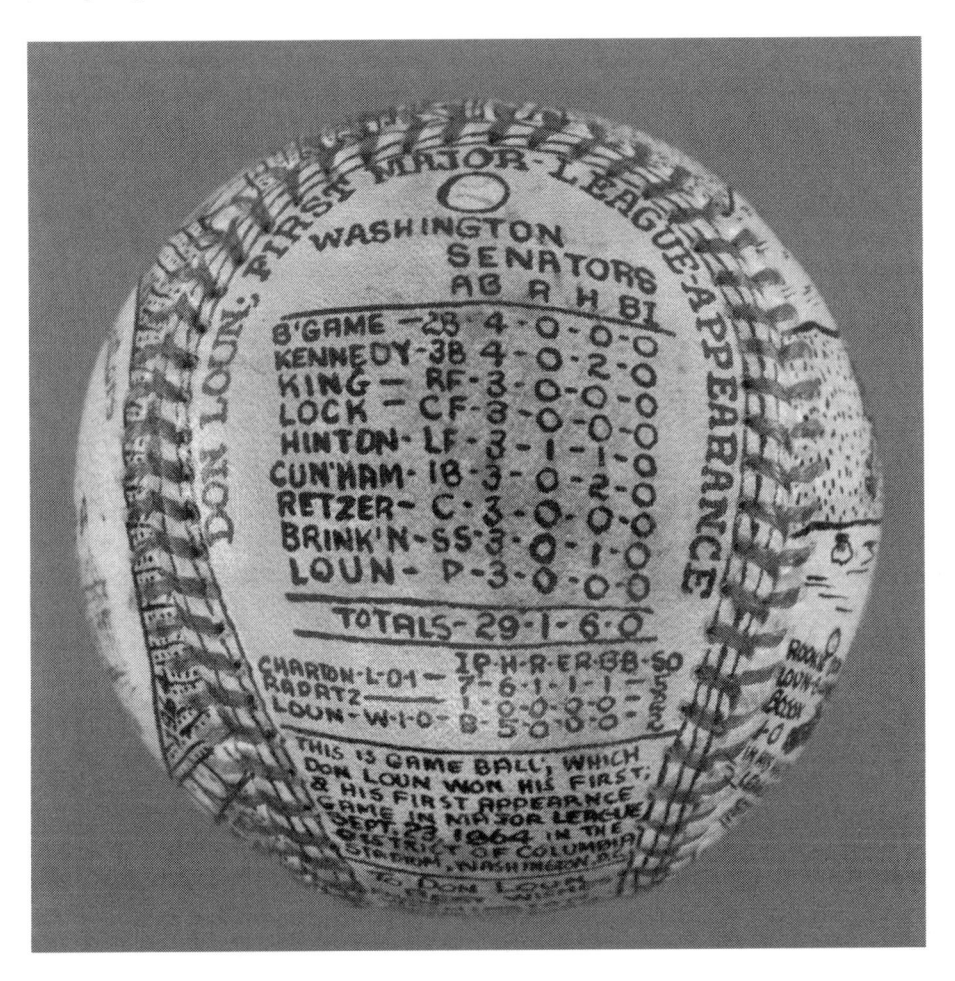

Painted game ball from my Major League debut (9/23/64), showing team lineups and scores

Major League Shutout

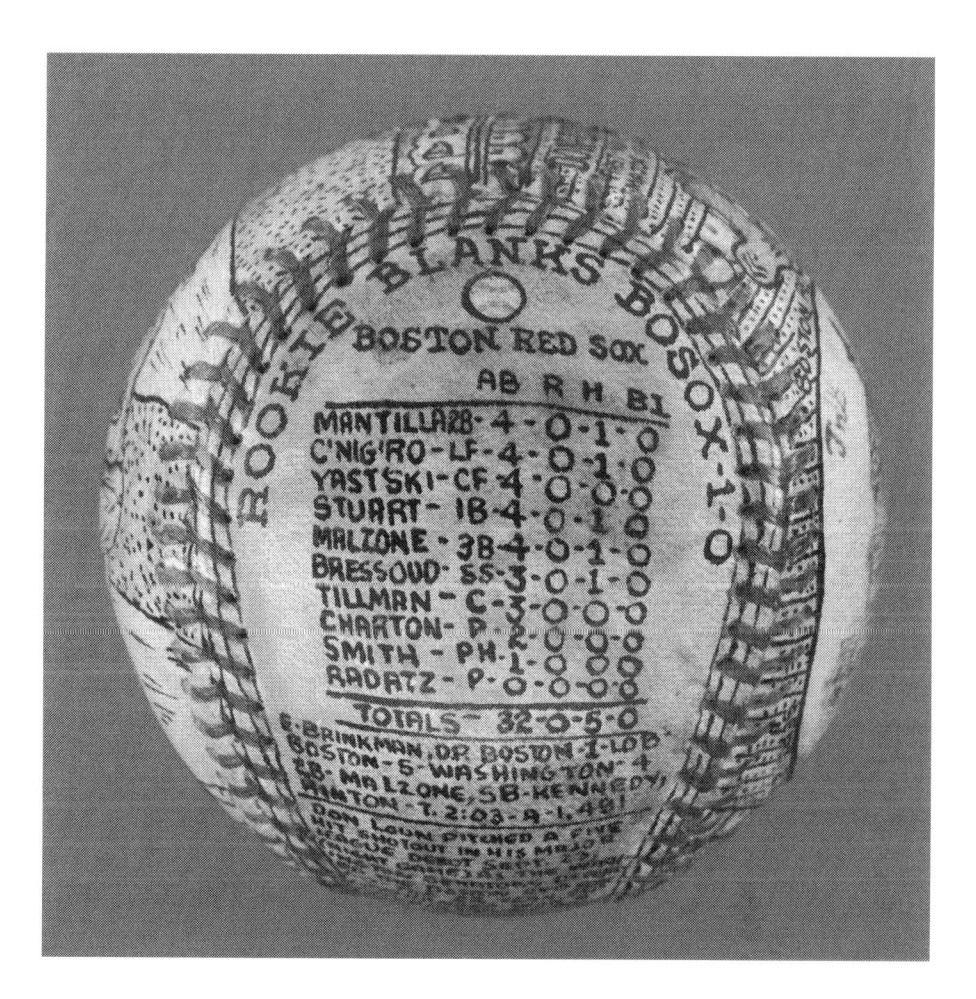

Management was huddled together and nodded as I walked by. The first comment by one of them was, "You only threw two fast balls all night and only struck out two."

Wow. I was silent. WTF.

> It had been about two hours and 17 minutes of complete concentration with 92 pitches.
>
> I had thrown sliders, fastballs, and change ups all evening for strikes. There were no walks. I was effective

with all of my pitches with no foolish mistakes. There were two fast balls—Yes! Those two extra-fast fast balls prevented two runners in scoring position from advancing. The fast balls were fast enough to accomplish my goal. Would more strikeouts and fast balls have had a better outcome?

I was in control of my game.

Plus, Kim Retzer called one hell of a game! He knew how good my change up was, so he called it instead of fastball after fastball. Well done!

If any young, hungry sports writer had wanted a story that could play well with young men and women everywhere, this was one. You have to be a little bit lucky and have people see the possibilities. The press can help you with encouraging, positive articles, or they can hinder you by lack of recognition of your achievements. It could have been a much bigger story for everyone.

A surprise ending after the game occurred when Jim Lemon came up to me in the locker room. He presented me with a sack of money, and said, "Lefty, here is your $25 fine. You won't find any of the bills that you left with me. It's all coins. I even had the quarters changed to pennies so you have a good collection of pennies to start with."

He laughed, and we looked at each other, and both laughed.

Jim then congratulated me on my performance that evening. He admitted that the bus had left a little early in that game back in Williamsport and that is why he returned the fine. I was reminded that arriving only a few minutes early may not be early enough. Jim had been one of my favorite managers. It was a good ending to my day!

48

NEW GEAR

Click, click, click, clack, click, click, clack!

That's all you could hear coming down the hallway. The player was mumbling to himself, "What's wrong with the spikes? They are too long. These are new shoes and I never should have worn them."

It was kind of funny at first but when I reflected on it, I realized that could really ruin your outing experience. I made a mental note to not wear new spikes. I don't recall the outcome of his game, but he wasn't happy with how it started out—all because of new spikes.

In another unrelated story, a teammate tried out a new glove. The very first ball that was hit back to him flipped out of the glove, flew over his head, and landed on the ground. He knew instantly he had made a mistake by using the new glove. It was probably not the best decision to use new gear before breaking it in. It was always good advice to have two pairs of shoes, two gloves, and a spare of anything that could cause a problem.

Major League Shutout Debut

It was automatic to avoid mistakes. Sometimes we had to admit that it just wasn't our day. Perhaps the umpire squeezed the pitcher or whatever the problem might be. If the pitcher and catcher conversed afterwards, they might find out the pitches were bad, or the umpire was having a difficult day himself. I actually had my catcher tell me that the umpire told him that he was having a rough day and apologized. Charlie Keller II had warned me that that might happen.

All pitchers could do was roll with it. Our job was to get the batters out. We had to make whatever adjustments where necessary and not create new problems. As a rookie, I had NO EXCUSES.

49

BIG LEAGUE BANTER

My pitching debut was two days before the Yankees came to town for a weekend series. I had a good workout the day before and was just sitting in the dugout watching the Yankees warm up. The Yankees were having a great season and were in position to clinch the American League pennant for the 14th time in 16 years.

Don Zimmer, our catcher, was standing on the dugout steps. Mickey Mantle yelled at Zimmer, "Hey Zim, why didn't you hold that rookie to pitch until we came to town. You know how much we like young pitchers."

Zimmer glanced over at me and mumbled something like, "I don't make those choices."

Elston Howard, Yankee catcher, was warming up Whitey Ford and he kept dropping the ball and scratching it on the ground before he threw it back to Whitey.

Major League Shutout Debut

Someone yelled to Howard, "Why don't you box me a crate of oranges? You don't drop them on the ground when there's someone on base."

Howard just grinned and didn't acknowledge anything.

This banter could have gone on all night. This ragging was typical among teammates and opponents, with no ill will intended. It's those moments that make baseball great without really trying. It's impulsive. You ride one guy, turn around, and get three or four other guys involved. That's the camaraderie you miss when you leave the game. There are stories that have been told that just develop in the heat of the moment, the exchange, and the respect you have for each other.

Don Zimmer had a great sense of humor, was a helpful teammate and consummate professional. I had a lot of respect for him. He was called up to the Big Leagues from coaching Winter Ball because management thought he could help the pitching staff by learning to catch. He had previously caught ball games, but there was a training process and they wanted to be reassured that he was comfortable.

When he left Washington, he went to the Yankees where he managed and coached from the bench. He was an overall instructor with the organization. When I asked him if any of the joking was about real shenanigans, he rolled his eyes and said, "Rookie, there's a lot to learn up here."

I was always learning something new. The next series was with Baltimore. The rookie rule came back into play as Gil Hodges was not going to start me against Baltimore. It would have been a perfect time to start me because I was from Maryland and had performed well and deserved a chance to pitch. In fact, I could have started or pitched in relief in at least five games, including the Baltimore game.

Baltimore was currently leading in the American League, and surprisingly, was drawing low attendance, and little press coverage. Maybe having a local boy make his debut with a contender could have done something to improve attendance. However, it was a rainy night in Baltimore and Lee McPhail, Baltimore GM, gave everyone back his ticket and offered a rain check. A classy move for him and a missed opportunity for me.

50

YOU HAD TO BE THERE TO SEE IT

During the ten days that passed after my debut, fellow teammate, Claude Osteen, asked me to show him how to throw my change up. Mine was a very effective change up and he had noticed. After one batting practice, I showed him my technique and he picked up on it quickly.

Finally! A chance to pitch again. It was October 3 in Boston at Fenway Park, The Green Monster. We had a ten hour bus ride to Fenway, where I could be a starter, reliever, or bullpen guy. Teammates taunted me and suggested I was going to be challenged differently than I had been in the four years that I had played because we were playing in Fenway Park. I was a left-hander and The Green Monster was going to "buggy whip" me. I was going to have green paint on my right shoulder. That is not what I wanted to happen. Team spirit was questionable.

Major League Shutout Debut

I was the starter. It was a very tight strike zone set up at Fenway. Home plate was a little too small for me. I would not use the 12 inch, down the cock pitch, unless I made a mistake. My control was very good for not having pitched for ten days. At Fenway you have 3 inches on the left and 3 inches on the right side of home plate, and I wasn't going there. That's the way it was and that's how it was going to be. I just had to deal with it. I was never going to show up an umpire. I never did it in all the years that I played.

I believe that the people who were in a position to know had an idea of how this game would turn out. During the game we noticed the increasingly tighter strike zone. The corners seem to be disappearing on the plate.

A slow roller was hit to the third baseman where it hit a rock or pebble. The ball bounced over the third baseman's head and stopped before it reached the outfield grass. When had that ever happened at this level?

As the game continued, a ball was hit to the shortstop with a man on first base. The shortstop fielded the ball, and at the same time, accidentally stepped on his own glove. The ball remained in the shortstop's glove, on the ground, as his momentum propelled him toward second base to make the play. It was an anticipated double play, but as it turned out, everyone was safe. The odds of stepping on one's glove, with the ball in the glove, was highly irregular at this level of play. Additionally, Carl Yastrzemski hit a routine fly ball toward right fielder, Willy Kirkland, who juggled the ball multiple times in front of the warning track, as it moved toward the low fence. It looked like he would juggle it out of the park for a home run, but he regained possession and got the third out.

We did not score a run. Boston won 7-0. I was charged with 4 runs and 3 errors. Carl went 0 for 7.

You Had to Be There to See It

After the game, John MacLean, sports writer and radio announcer, commented that my pitch location was solid. He came up to me in the locker room and said, "Lefty, here's your scorecard. I'll tell you what. You had to be here to see this one. I would never have believed what took place and, just like that, you were out of the ball game."

That's baseball and those things happen. My control had been very good for not having pitched in ten days. Charlie Keller II had told me there would be days like this. Truer words were never spoken.

51

DODGER INVASION

During the winter months of 1964, there had been some trades. Frank Kreutzer, a left-handed pitcher from the Chicago White Sox, joined the ball club at the end of the 1964 season. There were seven players from the Dodger organization and one pitcher from San Francisco, Mike McCormick. Pete Richert from the Dodgers was the main attraction because of the trade of Claude Osteen to the Dodgers. Gil Hodges came along with the package, as did Frank Howard, Phil Ortega, Doug Camilli, Mike Bromley, Dick Lines, and Nick Wilhite. Five left-handed pitchers. WTF.

Even though Spring Training wouldn't start until February 20, 1965 in Pompano Beach, Jim Duckworth and I wanted to get an early start loosening up. We began practicing in mid-January throwing at my hometown high school. Since we only had one mound to use, we did the best we could and were thankful to have skilled catchers. Billy Seidling, a catcher from

Frederick who later signed professionally with the Washington Senators, caught for us, along with another fellow. Billy went on to have a successful career in teaching, counseling and officiating sports. We both share the honor of being inducted into the Alvin G. Quinn Sports Hall of Fame in Frederick. It would have been great to have Jake Lenhart from Buckeystown catch with us also. Not sure where he was at that time.

Ducky and I headed to Spring Training together. We ended up going to a boat show where Ducky talked about going back to DC by boat after we made the team because he didn't like to fly. He thought he could skipper the boat and was very comfortable with that idea, but I wasn't. That wasn't going to happen with me. The most important thing for me was to make the ball club.

We stayed in the "Freddy Baxter Lodge," the locker room at the Pompano Beach ballpark. Freddie was one of the trainers who looked after our players. He arranged for about six of us to have cots to sleep on in the locker room for the two weeks before the rest of the team arrived. It was clearly not as luxurious as the Golden Falcon Hotel, where the team would soon be staying, but it was an expense we could afford.

We worked out every day doing what we had to do to get ready. We were fortunate to have some people to catch for us. I think Doug Camilli showed up along with another catcher who was below Triple A level. A few stragglers came in, but no one was really ready to pitch. Ducky and I shared some of the work in batting practice. Guys were working and throwing for five minutes but it wasn't really noticed. The guys under contract showed up and worked into the batting practice rotation and got their pitching in. There were a lot of pitchers trying to make the club from both the new Dodgers and us Senators.

Dodger Invasion

For someone like me, who was brought up through the Minor League system in the Senators organization, and was promised a shot during Spring Training, the situation was looking questionable. Gil Hodges, our new manager, said himself that it was probably a lot to ask to make the ball club. I guess there were things that Gil knew that some of us didn't know.

Players coming over from the Dodgers may have known more about what the odds were regarding the future for them with the Washington Senators organization, but I was not privy to any of that information. I heard that the Dodgers had expectations of a pennant win with Claude Osteen, the ace and 15 game winner with the Senators, the "cellar dweller." Leaving the Dodgers organization had to be tremendously disappointing but a Triple A log jam at the top might have existed. Some of the Dodgers who had been traded could have been optioned to almost any club.

Coming to Washington was lifeblood to the Dodgers. Washington was still an expansion club with several owners over a few years. There were some concerns that having our manager be an ex-Dodger might have given the Dodger players more comfort in making the club. I don't say that Gil Hodges was biased. I say that he had to be encouraged about some of the young Dodger arms he was getting along with the reputation that might have come with them. He may not have had much information about the young arms in the Senators organization. I never saw the Dodger pitchers actually pitch. They practiced on a different field and played against other clubs. It was as though we Senators were the B team, or, in a different league.

Did I know what was going on? NO!

I wasn't getting the work on a regular basis that I thought I should have gotten. I had worked for four years in the Minors and was ready to do what the managers and coaches wanted me to do.

Major League Shutout Debut

It seemed they weren't ready for me to do much of anything in the way of showing them how fundamentally sound I was. The pitching coach showed up and was having us go through the routine of how to field bunts and various things we had to do to cover bases, throw to bases, and make sure we didn't walk or balk. That was the beginning of this Spring Training workout.

As Spring Training went along I did not seem to be directed in any organized rotation ever. I never knew if I was going to pitch. It wasn't what I expected when I was told I would get a shot at making the club. Gil Hodges actually told a reporter that he was going to give me a good look. I don't know when that was going to happen.

Sid Hudson, the pitching coach, told six of us to head to the bullpen because he might need us in an exhibition game we were playing. As the game progressed, and with only two outs remaining, it looked like I would not get in the game. I began to stretch and loosen up. I just needed to throw because my arm had not gotten a workout, and I had been accustomed to a regular rotation. It was me trying to keep my arm exercised and tired. Hudson must have seen me because he showed up and told me to sit down because he still might need me in the game which was almost over. I needed to pitch, but did not get my chance to get in the game.

After coming to Spring Training two weeks early and working as hard as I did, it was all for naught because I wasn't being used and nobody seemed to care what I was doing. Hudson was acting as though he was angry with me, and all I could figure out is maybe somebody wondered why I was throwing when I hadn't been told anything ahead of time about being in the game.

Spring Training was not what I had expected. It was quite a disappointment.

52

DIAMONDS IN THE ROUGH

During my first Major League Spring Training, I met a very nice gentleman and his wife. He was one of the locals who wanted to get to know the new ball players in camp. Bill and his wife, Janet, owned a motel in Pompano Beach, Florida on the Intercoastal. They understood the pressures on young baseball players working hard to make a Major League team. Being with them was always relaxing, entertaining, and a great break from the grueling workouts. Bill was a storyteller and a colorful character.

We enjoyed fishing together and caught a lot of Spanish mackerel. On one outing, we were so successful we brought the Spanish mackerel to the chef at the Golden Falcon Hotel where the team was staying. The chef prepared the fish for all the ball players and hotel guests. It was fresh, delicious and a memorable feast.

Major League Shutout Debut

Bill was a professional skin diver. He dived off the Intercoastal for lost belongings, especially for those who were inebriated or lost their false teeth overboard, so he told us. I found that image quite humorous. Jim Duckworth and I enjoyed relaxing at his home, sipping iced tea, and listening to his stories after a tough day of fundamental drills.

On Tuesdays Bill would go to a motel on the strip in Pompano Beach and entertain the elderly ladies by weaving them Panama hats. He climbed up palm trees using ankle braces, and harvested palm branches. The ladies chose the style hat they wanted and a week later he would return with a lovely Panama hat. If anyone left the area, he and his wife mailed the hats to the address given.

Bill had played a role in the movie, <u>Tony Rome,</u> with Frank Sinatra. Sinatra was supposed to be a skin diver, but Bill was the actual diver in the movie. I have watched that film and he was, indeed, a professional diver, without question.

Years later, when I was shuffled off to Buffalo, Casey Cox and I happened to be in a bar where the hockey players hung out. Who walked in? Bill Arsenal. He had navigated a boat through the locks into that particular area. It was good to see a friendly face from better days. Unfortunately, my career was not going well in Buffalo.

With the pressures that existed in Spring Training, it was nice to know such a nice couple as the Arsenals.

53

A TRAPPED MOUSE

The sun was out during all day practices. At the beginning of the season we had two sessions per day. Later, we switched to one-a-day practices, except for the guys who wanted extra hits. Some guys would shag just to be on the field. We had no formal rules and regulations set up about curfew. Normally, it was set at midnight, and that would be something that was usually discussed, but hadn't been discussed this season. It was as if they wanted guys to break the rules and then they would deal with that accordingly. It would just add another asterisk beside a player's name.

What happened at 10 o'clock one night when I was in bed was that I got a call from two of the veterans on the team. They got together to harass me out of the hotel with call after call after call, wanting me to meet them in the lobby. They wanted to go out to The Mousetrap, a nearby nightclub. After about the fifth or sixth call, I gave in and joined them.

Major League Shutout Debut

There were a lot of ex Playboy Bunnies who were there to meet ball players. All the girls we met on the Intercoastal were aware of each others' connections with various ball players. Some of the Bunnies were still working and my teammates knew some of them from Dodger days and the switch back from the Minors so it was a pretty social evening. One of the ladies drove us back to the hotel where we saw Hodges and a couple of coaches coming out of the hotel bar, which was off-limits to the players.

The veterans got out of the car and walked right by Hodges and the coaches. Hodges ducked behind the cars in the parking lot to spy on who was still in the car. It was me.

I directed the driver to quickly back out of the hotel parking lot and dump me off at the nearby beach, as I did not want to be noticed. I hurried back to the hotel and slipped inside, undetected.

Everybody and Uncle Louis were hustling on the field at practice the next day. Hodges had noticed that the team was concentrating and working hard. Therefore, at 1 o'clock when we split for lunch, he said, "There will be no afternoon practice today. You guys were really giving it a good go, and I want you to know I noticed."

As he dismissed us he added, "Wait a minute. There were some guys out last night. You know who you are. Stop by my office. Some of you don't know, but if you are going to be out late, you need to leave me a note in the coach's box or at the hotel so everybody knows where you are."

That was the first I had ever heard of that rule. We had never done that in the Minors anywhere that I played. I was caught, and that was the way it was going to be. I went to his office repeatedly, but he was so busy with other players, it took a while before I finally was called.

He asked me to sit down and questioned, "What are you doing in here?"

A Trapped Mouse

I answered, "I was out last night."

He laughed and said, "Yeah, I bet you were the guy that went down by the beach and came up. You know that's exactly what I would have done if I had been out."

He added that he knew I didn't know the rules, but it didn't matter. He reminded me that we were all in it together and there would be a fine. We needed to be protected so that if someone saw us out, they wouldn't create a private story that could be incriminating.

He concluded, "You might like to know that 19 guys preceded you in here. There were a lot of guys out last night."

He knew Minor League players didn't have much money. Therefore, he indicated I could pay the fine as soon as I was able. Those two veterans never spoke to me the rest of Spring Training—maybe feeling a little guilty? Maybe not!

54

MONTEZUMA'S REVENGE

During Spring Training we had a game in Mexico City. When we landed at the airport, everyone already knew about the water: Don't drink the water unless it is bottled.

Unfortunately, bottled water was scarce. At the airport, one of our players handed me a cup of lemonade. He said he got it out of the machine, but it was in an open cup. In my view it may have had local water in it, but no one said anything, so I drank it. Coaches Rube Walker, Joe Pignatano and Sid Hudson may have had a feeling about it but no one said anything. I always wondered about Sid and myself not working well together. He had demonstrated how to throw a curve ball during Winter Ball using a gadget he devised. I was unable to throw using his device, and that may have made him less interested in me.

Major League Shutout Debut

Not long after we arrived in Mexico and were walking through the terminal, we spotted teammates Steve Ridzik, Ron Klein and Don Zimmer walking three abreast wearing extra large Mexican sombreros. They were walking six feet apart so their sombreros would not touch each other, whereby taking up the width of the concourse. They were definitely the "three amigos" strutting through the terminal with their sombreros bouncing up and down rhythmically. We didn't see them again until we got to the hotel. I wished someone had taken a photograph.

I remember the ride from the airport to the hotel. There were many beautiful buildings and colorful murals. Surprisingly, there were archaeological ruins being excavated downtown near our hotel. I thought that kind of excavation would have occurred years earlier. Maybe those ruins were part of the ancient Aztec civilization.

That evening I began to feel poorly. My stomach ached and I was sweating profusely with chills and dysentery. The three coaches stopped by and had the hotel doctor take my temperature which turned out to be 104 degrees. The coaches informed me they wanted me to start the game the next evening. I knew I couldn't make the club in bed and I wanted to make sure they used me, so I needed to be ready, and I had until the next evening to improve. The coaches wished me well and said they would check back to see how I felt in the morning.

Overnight was miserable. Chills. Fever. No sleep. The next morning the coaches came to check on me.

I said, "I gotta pitch. I cannot make the ball club if I'm in bed."

I had all day to recover and rest before the night game.

When I pitched that night in Mexico City, it was like taking a pig to the slaughter. I was dehydrated, sweating all the day before, all night and day, and during the game. I definitely had a good bout of Montezuma's Revenge. I asked for it. I don't remember much about it but I know it was a disaster.

My lackluster performance in Mexico was what the coaches saw. The fans had a good time heckling me. I had barely gotten to the dugout and the pillows that they brought along were flying out onto the field.

It was so unfortunate that I had enjoyed such a hopeful spring, this was my opportunity to shine, and it was a disaster. I should never have pitched.

When I got back from Mexico, it seemed like there were designs on how things were going to happen, and I often wondered if there was some kind of conspiracy by some of the players. We were all trying to make the team and there weren't enough positions for all of us. I had four years experience. I was on the timeline to succeed. People were saying there was something in the works as to the information the coaches and managers had that was going to set up how many left-handers, and which left-handers, might be able to make the club. The others had to work their way into it, and that was what they were prepared to do.

There wasn't enough room for seven or eight left-handed pitchers. Without question, one or two starters would have been the extent of it. No one had the vision of using four or five left-handed pitchers. We proved in Pensacola that it was something that needed to be looked at because it was successful.

Were they going to give all the right-handed players in the league an advantage over the left-handers who were going to start? Were they not going to see any right-handed pitching? It's no advantage one way or the other if they're all dynamite players. Then there would be more of an emphasis on two or three left-handed starters at most. No one even had the vision of only two lefties. That was pretty much throughout the league that one left-hander would be in the starting rotation. There would be either a five-day starter, or a six-day starter, who would be a left-hander.

The most frustrating part of Spring Training was that there were no meetings or shared information. The coaching staff seemed unapproachable. Gil Hodges was definitely the bear in charge. Hodges was going to make the ball club the way he saw fit because he was Club Manager now. Selkirk was General Manager and should have had input, but I'm not sure how much he had. He was strong-headed and had come from the Yankee organization. They didn't call him "Twinkle Toes" for nothing. He earned that name because he was a hustler. He was a smart individual, and he was the right man for the job at the time. Hodges was a noted name and there was quite a difference between George Selkirk and Gil Hodges. The Farm Director would have been the lowest influential individual. Even the managers from teams of any Minor League players would be consulted if they happened to be at Pompano Beach. We never knew who was in the running to be called up because management never let us know.

The Mexico City fiasco was still in my rearview mirror, but I kept working to regain my rhythm. I had a chance to pitch against Houston where, unfortunately, I slightly hyperextended my elbow early in the game. I pitched well enough to keep us in the game. However, I certainly did not impress anyone. Afterward, I was on the shelf for about 10 days. I had overthrown a curveball, and it took its toll. I was struggling and needed something: encouragement, suggestions, or reassurance. Some notice by the coaching staff might have made a difference, but that did not happen.

At the end of Spring Training I was optioned to Triple A Hawaii, a world away from where I wanted to be.

55

ALOHA!

Aloha! As we arrived in Honolulu on Pan Am we had a very warm welcome, not only in temperature, but in hospitality. As we exited the plane lovely hula dancers placed fragrant leis around our necks. Hawaiian music played in the background. As we left the tarmac we were greeted by the Hawaiian Islanders' owners and staff. The newly formed Triple A baseball team had just aligned themselves with the Washington Senators organization. Group and individual photographs were taken. It was quite a celebration for both the Hawaiian Islanders, and us.

My good friend and roommate, Carlos "The Chief" Medrano, who would later be the best man at my wedding, and I, roomed together along with Dave Hertz, a third baseman. We had a starting pitcher, a reliever, a closer, and a third baseman in one efficiency! It was expensive but we were only going to be there every two weeks or so, and it was not that uncomfortable.

Major League Shutout Debut

Me and teammate Carlos "The Chief" Medrano arriving in Honolulu, HI, 1965.

Our place was on Namahana Street, about 10 minutes from the Waikiki Beach Hotel, and near the Gaslight Club and Hotel Honolulu. The Ilikai Hotel was a brand new, fully air-conditioned hotel where the team stayed the first two weeks. It was all complimentary so we had a chance to get around town. We walked to most places but often had locals show us around. We checked out handmade crafts and relaxed at Waikiki beach. The slower pace of everyday activity was refreshing. We enjoyed eating at Fred and Frank Kaneshiro's Columbia Inn and listening to Don Ho, who sang nightly at Duke Kahanamoku's International Market Place. Every now and then a case of pineapple would show up at the hotel for us. The USS Arizona was in the harbor, unfortunately, still leaking oil from the disaster at Pearl Harbor in 1941.

We started our workout schedule two weeks before the season opened in Hawaii. Our training in Hawaii was different than it was on the mainland. The brutal sun was unforgiving. If you went to sleep on the beach and spent any time beyond 15 minutes out of the water you would pay with a painful sunburn. We were very well schooled on how to handle it and what it meant to be the home team in Honolulu. Not only were the folks fantastic, but it gave us a distinct advantage of how to handle the climate. You could almost count on a very misty shower at 4:00 p.m. every afternoon.

Our days began at 8:00 a.m. with breakfast at the ballpark. We started by working out fundamentally: getting familiar with the diamond, the ballpark, the stadium, and the wind changes. Everyone made the needed observations. Occasionally, we got trade winds, but not anything that caused us to be uncomfortable, or need to wear a jacket. If we wore a long sleeve sweatshirt, that would be fine. We worked out for about 3 hours and then broke for lunch around 12:30 pm or 1:00 pm. We worked on fundamentals all morning. Guys were in the hitting cages whenever they needed to be, catching fly balls, or working on the team double play at second. Pitchers threw to the different bases working on basics: fielding bunts, playing pepper, hitting fungos, lining up throws from the outfield to the various bases, and backing up the line. It was similar to Spring Training.

Major League Shutout Debut

About 3:30 p.m. that routine would start to fall off and certain pitchers would be finished with their work. They may get up for batting practice and shagging which lasted most of the afternoon. Also, the afternoon might include an intrasquad game where we would play a regular game of four or five innings. We focused on lining up, throwing to the cutoff man, and throwing to the bases. Anything that was scouted was reviewed in the shady bleacher section. What we did depended on how everyone was putting their time together. If it looked like players were building strength and there was not a problem, the coaches would leave the players in the sun for a period of time. They did not want to drain us and that was just part of why you had baseball caps. You weren't working on a tan, you were paying attention to what the game was going to call for. Those days started to have shorter workouts because of ball games. We sometimes had practice games when we could pick up college players. Meanwhile, owners were busy selecting ball boys and other staff.

George Case was the manager and told us to be watchful of what we were doing after hours. He reminded us to stay out of the press. Reporters weren't looking for any trouble, they were just curious as to who was there, where they came from, and what they thought about Hawaii. Every once in a while there was an interview on TV. Players were invited to go on the radio describing what was going on when light cameras would be out. It got to be secondhand, but we were usually out of the ballpark between 4 and 5 pm.

Everyone was curious about what everyone else was doing after hours. Guys shared different tales of where they met Miss so-and-so. The Chief jokingly searched for Miss Honolulu, but she wasn't there! She was in Portland, Oregon. He eventually met his future wife in York, Pennsylvania. She came out to Hawaii, where they were married at home plate!

Aloha!

In our two weeks on the road, in Portland, we played a three or four-game series, depending on the weather. Occasionally we played a full nine innings. Split doubleheaders where the folks left the ballpark and then returned for the second game were common. The second game had a new admissions fee. That was the first time I had really experienced that. It was pretty popular in areas where heavy rains were, compared to the East Coast, where we just played seven-inning doubleheaders, and the fans stayed in the ballpark.

After hours life got to be very interesting. I must admit that we were treated to every luxury I think that Hawaii had to offer. My roommate had a chance to go to Maui but missed an evening game. I wasn't interested in going anywhere because I wanted to be where the ball club was. Pitchers could be a little more flexible if they had pitched a lot. We were looking for an extra day's rest, which could be discussed with the manager. Coaches needed to know where players were going and when they would be back. The club had an escort for the players in Maui, or transportation if players went to the other islands. Maui was the easiest island to visit, and where families generally went when they came to visit. Hawaii was a genuine paradise.

56

ROYAL TREATMENT

*H*awaiian fans were a bit different than baseball fans on the mainland. As the games began with a packed house, we first timers noticed how quiet the stadium seemed to be. Then, all at once, as the players ran onto the field, the fans roared like bulls charging matadors and tossing them into the air. When the action picked up, so did the noise. I think it was partly because they were not excited during the game. It was almost like watching a golf match. Fans talked, but in a very low murmur.

It was hard to adjust to how persistent fans were in wanting our autographs. Every night we were in town they knew exactly where to wait for us. Players might sign at least 50 autographs when we had the time.

Frequently, we slipped out of the stadium a different way if we were in a hurry.

The trainer might say, "Well, there's no one over here. You guys may want to get out and get something to eat."

Major League Shutout Debut

If we went out the side gate, we might see fans. We felt guilty if we did not stop because the Hawaiians loved all of us.

The Hawaiians loved to host us after the games. They took us out as often as we would let them. Most of us saw the same people and they would talk about the game afterwards. If we went to a restaurant they would often go along. We liked going to smorgasbord restaurants that served mostly fish, but also had different kinds of meat. On special occasions restaurants hosted luaus, served with delicious salads, complete with a roasted pig that had been smoked all day in the ground, covered with palm leaves and hot rocks.

The most unusual place my roommates, The Chief, Dave and I went while in Hawaii, was a restaurant that locals, as well as ball players, frequented. The hostess had the distinction of being referred to as "The Queen Bee." She was friendly to everyone as she circulated among the tables and booths. It was common to sit at the same booth or table and have the same waitress.

Rumor had it that on a particular day or on a special evening, a waitress might bestow favors on the clientele that she had been serving. That was routine in this particular restaurant. When the waitresses took the job they said that they knew that that could happen, but they were still in charge of who they went with, or if they went with anyone. That had been common long before the Pacific Coast League came to Hawaii. It was unique because everyone had mutual respect and the girls were charming. They had very dignified manners and were beautifully dressed. We didn't hear that story until we had been with a group of three local guys who loved to go out after the game and talk baseball. After we had been out a few times with the guys we accepted that the restaurant was special to Hawaii.

As hard as we worked to improve our baseball skills, we found time to explore and appreciate Hawaii and its special baseball fans.

57

GREAT BALLS OF FIRE

Rain, rain, and more rain. It was a frog strangler. The game was canceled before our arrival so we were looking for something to do in Tacoma, Washington.

Hertz, Medrano and I learned that Jerry Lee Lewis was filling in for Jack Greene, a country singer. We hurried to the hotel front desk to see if we could get tickets, but sadly heard the show was sold out. The hotel manager mentioned he had a couple of reserved tickets that he planned to use. Reluctantly, he agreed to sell them to us at face value.

The theater was already rocking with typical country music when we arrived. Jerry Lee was scheduled to come on soon, so the usher hurried us to our seats, which turned out to be upfront, practically on top of the piano. Everyone in the theater stood, squealing and cheering, as Jerry Lee Lewis sauntered across the stage, rolled his cowboy boot across the piano keyboard, and yelled, "Okay folks, you've seen the rest, now you're going to hear the best."

Major League Shutout Debut

I had seen him have the same introduction on TV, but this was in person, and we were right in front of him! He threw back his chair, and tickled those piano keys for over two hours. It was thrilling to see one of the better entertainers of the day. He didn't want to quit. The crowd was clapping and cheering, encouraging him to continue. Everyone ignored the flickering lights that reminded us this show should have already ended.

I always enjoyed Jerry because he was a rogue. When he was in the Maryland area, he had the reputation of breaking up every piano that he ever used if it was a bit out of tune. He would "give it hell." I saw him again in a live concert, and he had the same energy and excitement as the one I saw in Tacoma— Great balls of fire! Great show!

58

I CAN'T HELP MYSELF

My first road trip from Hawaii to Indianapolis was more memorable than I could have imagined. My mother, brother and good friends were with me for their second visit since I started playing professional baseball. Management in Hawaii had made arrangements with the hotel to have a Hawaiian lei presented to my mother upon her arrival. It was a surprise for both of us. She looked like a princess and felt like one also! That was great for her because she had been having an extremely bad year.

We had a very special night at a fabulous restaurant. After dinner, we asked for a suggestion of where to go for entertainment and the staff mentioned a nightclub called The Birdcage.

When we arrived at The Birdcage we heard music that was recognizable but we weren't sure who it was. It turned out to be the Four Tops. They had a pause in their schedule and knew the owner of this club, so he asked if they would play a set. If word had gotten out that the Four Tops were performing it would have been bedlam, but instead, it was comfortable. I was with my brother Bob, Roy Hiltner, my mother, and Carlos. All at once we heard the song "I Can't Help Myself." That single was shooting up the charts and every one of us had heard it before.

The Four Tops paraded around the club singing while the patrons went crazy. Everyone loved it—-all ages! The audience stood and applauded the Four Tops when they finished singing. Within seconds, they returned for an encore!

The club manager asked the crowd to donate a little money to thank them for their efforts. Everyone in the club lined up and put their own money in the pot that was circulating. Imagine that night in a small club in Indiana.

The first time my mother and friends had visited me during my baseball career was in Pensacola in 1962 just before I got my notice to join the Army. This visit posed a different set of circumstances. My family had just built and moved into a new home the year before and I hadn't seen it yet. On this trip I was trying to make the big club and it hadn't happened. My mother had recently suffered a nervous breakdown, and, she and my stepfather had separated. After being only a year or so in their new home, they were losing it.

I found out later from Chuck Cottier that losing the home could have been avoided if the organization had known. I had no idea they might have helped. I learned that the organization could have made the payments and deducted the money from my pay. We could have worked it out or taken out a loan. There wasn't that much owed on the house because we owned the land, but it was traumatic.

Additionally, the previous fall, I thought I had everything in order to move to the Majors. I had signed a Major League contract and had gotten my bonus money, of which I gave most to my mother. I never knew there had been a problem with the house. I wished I could have helped.

The club wanted me to work on pick off moves and another pitch. After the last game in the Big Leagues, I had headed off to Winter Ball. So much had been going on at home that I never knew.

I'm glad my mother had that wonderful night in Indianapolis. She seemed like a different person and was just feeling great about things again. It was one of the best nights of our lives. I never thought such a wonderful time was possible considering all the drama that was going on at home and in my baseball career.

59

LOWLIGHTS OF HAWAII

Looking closely at 1965, I was seeing a future that was different than what I had anticipated. It looked as though it was going to be a tough year to pitch in the Pacific Coast League and why it was so different is hard to put together again. It's tough dredging up bad memories.

My main focus was trying to get back to the Big Leagues and that's what I had strived to do as my record shows. 1965 was my first losing year with a 6 and 12 record and an ERA of over 4.0. The number of hits and walks were significantly higher but the other side of that was there were some very well pitched games that I should have been able to build on. The only injury I had was a 10 day layoff due to a pulled oblique muscle. As usual, I rested and recovered fully.

The player of the month plaque that is in my home office hardly conjures up memories of how well I might have been playing. The large teak salad bowl I have also has a plaque that reminds me that I was chosen player of a homestand series. Had there been significant coaching with an interest in getting me back to the Big Leagues it could have made a difference. The catchers who were there were not familiar with me with the exception of Joe McCabe, and that was out of the Mexico spring training fiasco where Montezuma had gotten his revenge.

My recollection of 1965 was that there were frequent short outings of four innings each, a routine that was the reverse of what I was accustomed to. I was training the same way I had always trained, nothing was different in that regard, but four innings was not enough to keep my skills at the level I had previously found success.

Another area that could have affected my year was hydration. I was not accustomed to drinking a lot of water in the daytime. I had pitched four years without dehydration being an issue. Maybe it was an issue, maybe not.

George Case, first time manager, had a plateful and did not really know me. I felt like there was nobody in my corner, noticing anything that could help or encourage me. I think the trade from the Dodger organization had a profound effect on those of us from the Senators' organization. My recollection is that some of us felt ignored throughout the next three seasons.

Of course, the 1965 season had the huge issue of added pressure that I put on myself. The enthusiastic Hawaiian fans made all of us want to do a better job every time we were out. It would have been helpful to have coaching to correct any problems.

My overall recollection is one of disappointment, confusion, and lack of support. Definitely the doldrums and a time I have clearly tried to block from my memory. I hated being sent to Hawaii even though it was a paradise.

60

GOOD TIMES

After I pitched one game of a doubleheader in Hawaii and won, I was invited to broadcast the color on the radio and TV of the second game. I never saw the TV but it was fun describing the ball players and what they were trying to accomplish. I recall that Howie Koplitz pitched the second game and won. The exposure of broadcasting by a player broadcaster informed the patrons about the game in a meaningful way, and gave insights into how the game was being played by both teams. I enjoyed broadcasting opportunities back in York, on the radio, as well.

That evening we heard neighbors across the lanai having a big time dancing and singing. It turned out there were three gorgeous ladies who had just returned from clubbing at Duke Kahanamoku's International Marketplace Nightclub. Those places were hangouts for the players when we were in town. Great music and great food!

Major League Shutout Debut

The treat we were given across the courtyard was very stimulating. I wanted to get some sleep after our big day following a two-week mainland series. but it was too hard to resist the show as they danced, and sang around their lanai. The view was great until they finally turned out the lights, except for a lone night light.

The next day we met the ladies downstairs at the laundromat and thanked them for the evening entertainment. They were very friendly and also interested in us. Ironically, one of the ladies actually worked for one of the radio stations in Hawaii.

We enjoyed a two week home stand until we hit the road again. This was one of the better memories of the days in Hawaii.

61

WIENER TRUCK

*A*colorful old horse joined us in Hawaii as a player/coach. He enjoyed a good time and was quite adventurous with the mixed drinks, especially the Mai Tai with 180 proof black rum. It was common for players to compete with each other about how well they could drink. We didn't do much of that in the Minors. We heard about it, but I wasn't interested in drinking after I got my lesson once in Winter Ball with mixed drinks. Instead, I celebrated with a few beers just like anyone else on rare occasions. We all needed to have clear heads because you never knew when it was your turn to pitch.

One night the old rascal was pounding a few at the Gaslight Club. In the parking lot was an Oscar Meyer Wiener truck. Not long after taking a straight shot of that 180 proof rum on a dare from some players, and winning the bet, the old fellow got up to leave. Some of the players ventured outside with him and saw the wiener hotdog truck, slightly bigger than a Volkswagen. It was one long hotdog in a bun. The old rascal was feeling no pain and challenged the younger guys to raise the truck. Everyone grabbed a part of the truck and lifted it up. It was just about to fall on its side when they lowered it.

Suddenly, the old guy said he thought he could lift it by himself, and of course, everybody challenged him, betting he couldn't do it. With some difficulty, he managed to lift it, but it tilted over to one side and slightly damaged the chassis. He won the bet, but lost overall.

The driver of the truck had heard the ruckus, rushed out of the club, and immediately called the police. The wiener truck driver was upset because he was responsible for his truck. The police said that they would figure out what happened. They questioned everyone and concluded that the damage was minimal and the ball club had insurance that could cover any repairs. The police said they would issue a citation. Everyone hoped it would be a light punishment because many pounds of hotdogs had been sold that evening at the game.

At the ballpark the next day, we learned the consequences. The whole club had to run extra wind sprints after practice. It was typical for everyone to endure the punishment, even if they were not involved. The old fella was doing the sprints, but slowing down every time he got to centerfield. He threw up along the way, obviously not feeling well. Guys were watching him as they finished their workouts.

He said, "Boys, this is a lesson for you. You dance, you pay the piper. I will be here till they tell me I'm finished." Nobody was really angry at him because we enjoyed his quirky ways. It was tough, but we were thankful it was on a day off from playing ball.

Finally, the manager said that the old rascal could stop running. The rest of us had already stopped, showered, and were watching the old timer run. He didn't stop when he was told.

Wiener Truck

He said, "I think I have more to do and if you give me the OK, I'll finish when I finish."

The manager liked that attitude because he was an old timer himself. He thought the old fellow was setting an example for the younger players to be aware that when they step out of line they might need more "suffering" than everyone else. The trainer was told to keep an eye on him to make sure he was okay. We learned the next day that each time he ran one length of the field, he picked up a pebble and put it down on the other end of the field. Nobody really noticed that he was bending over and picking up something, but he did it to count how many laps he ran. We all learned a lesson along with him.

Occasionally, he would step in as a catcher, but he told us if he was in a game and we had a knock down situation that he would not try to stop a batter from coming at one of our pitchers. He said his fighting days were behind him.

He said, " It's your decision. You are on your own." He was a memorable fellow.

62

FRED VALENTINE

Freddy was one of the guys who came early to Hawaii from Spring Training in Baltimore or Washington. I wasn't sure which city because of the way Washington was divided. It seemed like he was owned by both clubs.

Everyone took a liking to him right away. He was very unassuming and quiet. The locals loved him because he was so accessible. They loved him also, or grew to love him, because he got the job done every day for 180 days. He put it out there and half those days were for the hometown club. He played his heart out both at home and on the road and I was blessed to see it. It was the best year I ever saw any ball player have in my nine years as a professional baseball player.

I thought I had seen quite a few good players, but he was the real deal. He was our lead off hitter, he could run through and steal bases, and he was a tough out. Everyone had to bear down for that first inning or he would not only make you throw strikes, but he would steal second, and third base, if you weren't careful. Normally, he was fully used in a hit and run situation against some pretty fair pitchers. We were not going to score a lot of runs, but Freddy was going to give us the opportunity to get on top early. Freddy was a dynamic player and a game changer. If he was on base, something exciting was bound to happen. After a game, he was spent, meaning he had left it out there, and win, lose, or draw, he was always the same in the dugout, and in the dressing room.

The best photograph I ever saw of a baseball player was of Freddy in front of our dugout, about 30 feet from the left infield foul line. As Freddy was about to score a run, he collided with the catcher, a hard slide, as usual. As captured in the photograph, Fred's grimace of fierce determination, contrasted with the catcher's painful collapse amid a cloud of shoulder height dust, captured a powerful image of Fred's strength and resolve. The photographer skillfully froze that image that I will remember forever.

At the end of the 1965 season, the Coca-Cola Bottling Company presented Freddy with a plaque, celebrating his extraordinary hustle. On the plaque were 52 silver dollars, one dollar for every stolen base. At the bottom of the plaque was a painting of the amazing photograph. It was a reminder of how he played the game; with hustle, all through his career.

He went on to the Big Leagues after that year. After baseball we got together, on occasion, with the Major League Ball Players Alumni Association, of which he was also a founding member. We played golf and visited at meetings until his death in 2022. My friend.

63

NEW WIND UP

Spring Training 1966 with the big club was lackluster. My oblique injury had healed long ago. I was playing well, but was not that impressive, as I recall.

The highlight of Spring Training was the annual Washington Senators Golf Tournament. The year before, I had finished dead last. This year I was teamed with Mike McCormick in this two-man event. We putted very well and ended up winning. A sports writer commented afterwards that if the Senators baseball team could play half as well as we played the golf tournament, they would have a winning season.

When Spring Training broke, I went back to Hawaii. One month into the season I was optioned to York in favor of Tom Cheney, and possibly Dave Stenhouse, and a couple of others. I was completely caught off guard by being sent down to Double A York. To add insult to injury, I found out while I was on the road in Spokane, Washington.

Major League Shutout Debut

Hawaii Manager George Case stated that I could be called up from York to Washington, as had been done by other pitchers. George stated that I was on the right road to getting back to my capabilities, and York would give me an opportunity to better my skills. I flew directly to York, never said a proper goodbye to the wonderful Hawaiians, and had no chance to get my belongings. Everything was mailed to me eventually, except the dry cleaning which I never got, because no one picked it up. It was only June. What a season this was going to be.

Surprise! Slow arm? Upon returning to York, I learned that I supposedly had a "slow arm." Nobody had ever mentioned that in Hawaii and I had never heard of the condition myself. York manager Billy Klaus, and Bert Thele, regional scout and coach, suggested I try a "no wind up" delivery. Might have been nice to have somebody mention it while I was in Hawaii.

Control was briefly an issue as I learned a new wind up. Warming up as a reliever took time with the new rhythm. With the work I was getting, my arm sped up and rhythm came rapidly. The new wind up was very comfortable and I had success. Soon I had my control back, possessed a no wind up delivery, and had the command of four pitches. The cutter was the last addition to my pitching repertoire. Harry Strom, Senators chief scout, told me I had a good selection of pitches and could be a regular starter, a spot starter, long relief, short relief, or closer in the Big Leagues. I had performed all of these roles since returning to York, and was capable of accomplishing all of them.

Location was key to my performance. Staying ahead of the hitters, fundamentally mixing pitches, and being able to throw most of my pitches at any time was in my repertoire because of my wind up improvement. Having bases on balls or walks against the opponent were frowned upon. I didn't find that to be a problem because walks never mean anything unless they score, and I was successful in throwing shutouts and shutout innings that far outweighed any slaughter time. Nobody ever had to worry. Getting me out of there or "he's going to get somebody hurt." That was not me. I had everything a pitcher needed except rest at that point.

My progression might have been compromised by new Washington manager Gil Hodges, who I found to be extremely fair, but also heavily reserved with his feelings. He had become a superstar and forever revered as a Brooklyn Dodger, and later, as a Los Angeles Dodger. In coming to the Senators organization it was easy to believe that he could have been biased, but not deliberately. I was not with the big club long enough to develop a meaningful relationship with him so my feelings were purely speculation in trying to understand what was happening with my career.

My control of pitches was quite complete but being in York was pretty discouraging. We had guys who couldn't catch fly balls, and may not have been able to hit their hat size. Our team had three no hitters thrown at them in one year. But we had to do what we could to keep the team close. I had gotten off to a pretty good start with long relief, short relief, and regular rotation. I felt like I was coming along pretty well with a new wind up. I had a new pitch where I turned over a screwball. It was reported that I was one of the best left-handed pitchers in the organization. With the new motion, the pick off moves, and my success, I expected to be called up in the fall of 1966 and invited to the Big Club Spring Training in 1967. Instead, disaster followed.

George Case, York manager in 1967, along with manager Billy Klaus, said I had been "selected" to go to Oklahoma City to join the Hawaii Islanders. A year earlier Case had told me to get better and assured me I would go to the Big Leagues. He added that

Major League Shutout Debut

Casey Cox had done that the previous year. I reminded him of his promise the previous year to send me to the Big Leagues.

He said, "You are moving up and that's what counts."

Promises made, but not kept.

64

SACRIFICIAL LAMB

*B*illy Klaus claimed I needed to go to Oklahoma City immediately. I had few details. Manager Terwilliger was short of pitchers and needed help. It had to do with military commitments. I had just pitched 7-8 consecutive days in York and was ready to go in the eighth game, the second game of a Friday doubleheader. I knew I was pitched out and needed three or four days rest. After the game I jumped in a car and went to Dulles airport and flew to Oklahoma City. I arrived around 10 PM Mountain time and went to sleep as soon as I could.

Soon after midnight I was called on the phone by Hawaiian Islanders Manager, Wayne Terwilliger. Of course it was about 2 AM East Coast time. Terwilliger wanted to know if I could pitch the next day, Saturday. I told him of my recent 7 to 8 consecutive days of pitching, including both ends of a Friday doubleheader. He firmly asked a second time, "I didn't ask you that. Can you pitch tomorrow?"

That felt like a loaded question. I could tell by his tone what he meant, and my reaction was automatic. He knew he had me in a spot *if I said "NO." That could have been a black mark on my file forever. I knew I needed to rest my arm, but I needed the support of management to authorize it, and that's not what happened. Saturday would be the 9th consecutive day I pitched. I had traveled at night, after having pitched, with virtually no rest. This was not Boot Camp, but that's how I felt I was being treated by this drill sergeant.*

The only thing I could say was, "You should know me, and I have never turned down a chance to start."

What I should have said was NO! I need four days rest. Didn't you check with Case, Klaus, and Selkirk?

What were the coaches, managers, and Farm Director doing? Nobody was paying attention to me. There was a definite lack of interest in what was best for me. There was no communication that made sense. I was told to go to Oklahoma City. It certainly wasn't about me. I was 100% prepared to go to the Major Leagues with proper rest.

This team had been on a losing streak. They had lost every game on the last road trip to the mainland. Pitchers were pulling Army reserve duty. Terwilliger was determined to reverse the trend.

About 14 hours after my conversation with Terwilliger, I pitched six innings to the top club, the Colt 45s, the Houston Astros Triple A farm club. They were 14 1/2 games ahead in the Pacific Coast League. I gave up one run, struck out six, and walked one. I had six solid innings which was more than I ever should have pitched.

After pitching six solid innings, I told catcher, Jim French, I thought I ought to get off the cutter because I was starting to cut it and it was biting me severely in the shoulder. I had been changing up all around and basically confusing the Colt 45s. Feeling pain if you are a pitcher was a red flag unless you had been doing it your whole career and got away with it. It was something that happened late in York when I had thrown in too many consecutive ball games.

Terwilliger heard me talking to French and hurried over. I planned to throw fastballs, change ups, and maybe show a slider. That was the kiss of death. He jumped up like a man who was about to be hanged if he didn't change the pitcher. He panicked and called Jack Jenkins from the bullpen. Instead of allowing me to go to the plate, Jenkins, my reliever, pinch hit for me immediately. We had been leading the ball game 3 to 1, and Jenkins proceeded to take the seventh inning. He gave up three or four runs and I got No Decision.

Harry Strom, our chief scout in the Pacific Coast League, came into our dressing room and complimented me on a great game against a really tough ball club.

He looked me over and said, "Lefty, you are going to the Big Leagues. You are going back!"

He added, "I just sent a telegram to Selkirk."

I was on top of the world. I was so proud and happy! FINALLY!

I didn't know it at the time, but GM Selkirk had made a decision to come to Tulsa which was the next stop on this road trip. He wanted to see me pitch there. I never knew much about George Selkirk, but I did know he had been an outfielder. I always thought the pitchers and fielders never really got along as outfielders never had much respect when it came to pitchers. But those were the guys who were calling the shots in the big leagues and were the managers.

Four days later, I was scheduled to pitch against Tulsa and I was hurting badly. I had loosened up after the Saturday night game by running hot water on my arm as I usually did both after a game and in the morning. This felt different.

Major League Shutout Debut

It was a sweltering 90° at 10 o'clock Sunday morning. I was excited because I was going to the Majors. I had a big breakfast, my favorite meal of the day, and was ready to rest my arm and get out of Hawaii. But the pain was still excruciating. It was like a hyperextension. Duckworth and I were playing catch and getting loose. I thought I could work it out and stretch it. It was hard to make any pain free pitches. The pain was like a mule kicking me in the shoulder.

At the ballpark in Tulsa I was trying to throw and I knew I was damaged goods at that point, or, at least, I knew something was wrong. I never had it before, but I knew that my arm really needed rest. After a short time on the mound, I took myself out of the game. I was optimistic, though, about coming back because I had done it before.

I let my arm rest and the trainer worked it out with a light rub. I could have had five or six days of just playing catch and stretching in the outfield, but I did not know that at the time. An examination by a doctor would have been the right thing to do. With proper handling I was a future Major League pitcher.

Pitching coach Sid Hudson should have been in on the discussion of the 8 out of 9 consecutive days that I pitched. No one was held accountable. Management worked together and took care of each other. I never had any dealings with Sid Hudson until that day. I felt like he couldn't help me when I needed it and that was his job. I was nothing more than a sacrificial lamb.

The only guy who really helped me get back on track was Billy Klaus. We worked together on changing the no wind up delivery. He got me working and back to pitching regularly or whatever they wanted me to do to build my arm. That was not a problem because I was always in shape.

After that game in Tulsa, Selkirk accused us pitchers of thinking we had to be 100%. He said it would never be that way and that we should get used to playing less than 100%. I doubt he knew what I had been *through for the past 10 days, but it really pissed me off because I certainly knew that we all played less than 100% healthy some of the time. This was not the ending I hoped for after working so hard for two years. Plus, it was the second time I had gotten back after being injured.*

I found myself trying to work out with my arm. No one was directing me on to how to recover. Instead, I was flying by the seat of my pants.

How could I use Charlie Keller's remedy to build up around the soreness just like a racehorse? I was pushing against door jams, working with my "Exer-genie," isolating the pain, and finally getting it to come around without any medication except Tylenol or Advil.

Following Tulsa, I was immediately sent back to York, unexamined. They didn't check me out in York either. The trainer's solution was Darvon. What was that? Nobody knew or nobody told me. Being reluctant to take the medication because I didn't know what negative effects it might have on me was possibly a reason to leave me alone and not do anything at all about my condition. Perhaps management was thinking they could option me out, that there would be some club who could look at the medical side. That was the only conclusion I could draw from the whole fiasco.

The lesson learned here was that I should never have pitched. I knew my arm needed rest. There had to be other pitchers available. I needed professional medical evaluation and care. I was used up.

65

CLOSE SHAVE

Late night check in did not mean everybody was tired and ready for bed. The team had just tripped into Elmira, New York, after midnight. We registered at our hotel, but the manager was upset because of our late arrival. Uniforms and equipment had to be taken off the bus and brought into the hotel. All the luggage had to be delivered to our 20+ rooms. Most of the hotel staff had left for the evening.

My arm was bothering me and I needed rest. I was still wrestling with the unfortunate turn of events that shut down my chance to go back to the Big Leagues. I considered myself along for the ride because there was little chance of me pitching. However, since no one was paying attention to me, who knows why I made the trip?

Players were starved and wanted to get something to eat before going to bed, but nothing was open. Quite a few of us headed to our rooms and went to bed. We planned to wait until breakfast to eat.

Major League Shutout Debut

Some die hard players just had to push it and go out on the town, which was not unusual. As soon as they got to a new town, they were looking for a bar or a place to hang out. This particular night, the effort was spearheaded by a new player who had just transferred in from another organization. He scouted out an open eatery where players could get a sandwich. So off they went about 1 AM.

When the players returned to the hotel, a giggly group of stewardesses was checking in. The new guy suggested the players watch the elevator to find out which floor the girls got off on. By listening for the girls' voices at each doorway they could identify which rooms had stewardesses.

All the commotion was atypical at this hotel especially since it was after 2 AM. After checking out where the stewardesses were staying, one player suggested the guys go back to their rooms and get cans of shaving cream and put it on the girls' door knobs.

It wasn't long before those of us who were sleeping were rousted out of our beds as a call had come from the hotel manager. He was furious that ball players were putting shaving cream on the doorknobs. The ladies were complaining that they couldn't get into their rooms because they couldn't turn the slippery doorknobs. The hotel manager yelled that he wanted us out of the hotel, and that the ball club was more trouble than they were worth!

Billy Klaus, team Manager at the time, called the Farm Director. He said it was urgent because the hotel manager was about to throw us all out. The Farm Director was the only guy who could probably save the day, which he did. He called the hotel manager and apologized profusely. We were told we were on the clock and anything additional that happened would get us kicked out.

Getting kicked out was not going to be an option. After 2 AM the likelihood of finding another hotel or motel that would accommodate over 20 ball players, staff, equipment, and luggage was highly unlikely. Billy said our only option would have been sleeping on the bus after we hauled all of our own belongings, uniforms, equipment, and luggage to the bus. We were fortunate the hotel manager gave us a second chance.

It was always a team effort, and if guys couldn't stay in control of other guys, then we would all suffer the same consequences. We had the responsibility to help manage guys who wanted to get out of control because it had a bad effect on all of us, and left a bad image on the organization.

We were thankful we did not have to leave the hotel. We stayed and kept the road trip intact and finished the series in Elmira, New York. I did not have to pitch. Now, what was next for me?

66

CHAOS?

I had been the overnight guy and they treated me like a red-headed stepchild. My arm was tired, drained and strained like never before. Neither Hawaii nor York were winning. My path to the Majors had been erased.

That irritates me to this day. I could have gotten back to the Big Leagues. I think I would have lasted at least four years. I was a credible left-handed pitcher. I threw 90+. I had three pick off moves. I had control of four pitches. Had they given up on me? Was anyone in management noticing me? NO, or, no longer.

I did what I could to regain strength and pitch again. I worked out every day in York. I ended the season throwing in the dark when the stadium lights were out. No invitation to Winter ball. No invitation to Spring Training.

Many years later, I learned that during this time period the Washington Senators ownership was changing with new owners, managers, and coaches. None of this reorganization was ever on my radar during the years I played. Could changes at the top have affected my movement in the organization? I don't know.

My winter season was spent fulfilling Army duty responsibilities. My military company had two weeks training in frigid Watertown, New York. The weather hovered around 21 degrees with outdoor camping. I know I could have had it a lot worse.

Following the dismal winter, I was assigned to Triple A Buffalo. Lo and behold, Wayne Terwilliger was the manager. He had lost the franchise in Hawaii. It was probably an expense management decided they could cut. It cost a lot less money to play in Buffalo than it would have been paying for clubs in Hawaii. I found out my roommate wouldn't go to Buffalo because of the cold weather. Smart guy. He did what was best for him.

I should have done what was best for me.

67

GAME OVER

Before I got to Triple A Buffalo in 1968, I heard that someone was pushing Terwilliger, which is maybe why he was pushing me. He was trying to salvage Hawaii at any cost. I was trying to get back. No one addressed my injury in York. I was told that Darvon was in the dressing room and the trainers said it would relieve the pain I was having in my shoulder. I probably needed to get it into my system but I was not interested. I decided if I needed drugs to play, maybe I shouldn't play.

For seven years in professional baseball, I had not used prescription drugs under any circumstances and I was uneasy about taking an unfamiliar substance. Plus, no one was able to give me much information about Darvon. I knew my work ethic, and the way I performed for seven years professionally without Darvon. If I couldn't get anybody out with my "stuff", then I certainly wasn't going to get them out with drugs.

Major League Shutout Debut

The few times I tried an over the counter pain reliever it never fully relieved my pain. Maybe I never gave it a chance. What I noticed was there was still pain when I was trying to get loose, going into a game, and while pitching. I needed someone official to talk with me about drugs. The trainer was not a medical authority. I wanted to trust that management would get me back on track.

Even though I wouldn't take Darvon, I didn't give up. I wanted to rebuild myself and I wanted to get back to the Big Leagues. My record was a dismal 0-3, but I pitched 53 innings with 37 strikeouts. I only gave up 9 home runs. The pain was constant, and it was clear, they had given up on me.

Years later, I learned that Darvon was an addictive opioid with many side effects. Following a number of drug related deaths, it was pulled from the market. A tough, but perceptive decision by me years earlier.

The following year I was optioned out to Houston, went to the Savannah Astros Double A, and ended up pitching for Manager Hub Kittle. He was a 70-year old guy who had managed for the Houston Astros. He was as repetitive as anybody I was ever around. Every night he would take us to the mound, whether we were young, or older. He went over basic information that every pitcher already understood. He wasn't as in-depth as I thought he might be. Maybe it was because he was old, or maybe it was just a task he was given.

Because of my shoulder injury, I missed the first road trip in my whole career. I finally got examined by a doctor and it turned out I had strained my back using my "Exer-genie", an upper body strength-building and resistance pulley system. I had gone to the ballpark to work out and had isolated the lower lumbar area with the "Exer-genie." In my effort to heal myself I had created more problems by overworking. I was unable to run or lift my knees up to run. When I got back to the park I tried running and it pulled me down.

Hub suggested I get treatment, get rested, and not go on the next road trip. Being in the pool, moving my legs, and relaxing my lower back muscle spasms, was what I needed. I ate pineapple for circulation. The trainers told me there was a pill made from pineapple, so eating fresh pineapple was on the right track. I still had hope I could reverse this setback.

The doctor said nothing about my shoulder. He told me it would take a while to recuperate my back and suggested I stay in a whirlpool treatment that included physical therapy and supervised swimming. He told me that if the ball club went out of town I should just go to the pool, hold onto the side edge, and kick my legs. He said that he wasn't letting me go without it. The doctor said, "I'm not releasing you. I want to make sure your back is right."

When the club came back from the road trip, I threw batting practice for 30 minutes. Afterward, a scout asked me how I felt. I said I felt good. A little later Kittle called me into his office and informed me that the club was giving me my release and that I could head back home as soon as I was ready. He said my obligation there was over. He added a derogatory comment that just solidified my acceptance of getting the hell away from there. I don't even know if they paid me my check. I hurriedly packed my gear and took the bus home.

It was the first time I wanted to be away from a ball club that was more interested in how high their socks were and what they looked like in their uniforms than they were in playing baseball and winning games. I heard later that Ted Williams had asked about me during Spring Training.

Major League Shutout Debut

Before I left town, the doctor who attended me in Savannah said he would send my information to a doctor in Maryland who specialized in vertebrae and herniated discs, and could further treat me. Technically, I could have hung in for the rest of the year, but the ball club was so bad I was fine getting away from them.

Encouraging me to use drugs that I did not feel comfortable with may have lengthened my career. It just wasn't worth it to me. Charlie Keller II had once told me that once it was over not to be a "hanger oner." If they want you, they know where to find you. Game over.

Part Three

OPINIONS AND INSIGHTS ON THE GAME

68

CHANGES

Does the game of baseball change from decade to decade, player to player, team to team, and location to location? From umpires to veterans to rookies, there are changes that are sometimes obvious and sometimes subtle. Here are some of my observations.

Is there a different strike zone for a hitter depending on whether he is a veteran or a rookie? Does a rookie pitcher have to prove himself? Watch and draw your own conclusions.

Wind direction and movement can affect players, especially pitchers. If pitchers warm-up in the bullpen that is housed within the stadium, their warm-up may be different than if there is a courtesy fence structure that allows the wind to be collected and rerouted around the ballpark. When a player comes in relief, it has a profound effect if he is not expecting the wind to be a factor. Wind problems are discussed beforehand. Wind characteristics in a stadium may affect how players are drafted, considering the position they will be expected to play. Think about Candlestick Park and Fenway Park.

Whoever talks about the drainage system affecting players? If the grass takes less water on one side, such as the first base line, rather than the other side, fielders and pitchers must adjust accordingly. The roll of the ball varies with the condition of the ground. How long or short the grass is cut on the infield can affect the speed of the ball in a bunt or ground ball situation. The way the grass is cut can be very influential for specific teams depending on who their position players are and how fast they move.

The strength of a team depends on being strong up the middle: pitcher, shortstop, center fielder, and second baseman. I never watched him regularly, but Ted Williams was probably better than most players in his day. If we looked at his stats we would recognize the Green Monster that players feared. Everyone, including opposing players, were more alert and thought about shifting a little bit when they played him.

A part of the game that seems to be missing today is that we do not bunt enough. We don't play to move the runners around. Ballparks used to be adjusted to the player. If you had a player playing third base and he wasn't agile, the batter might try him out the same way with the first baseman. Most of the time the first baseman will play deeper. If you give him an opportunity to get deeper, he'll go back there. All pitchers try to race everyone to first.

If a pitcher is 6'8", he throws downhill all the time. The umpire's zone should change, in my view. I think they should adjust depending on the pitcher's height. Shorter pitchers throw uphill. Mound height should be constantly in question. It's standard at 12 to 14 inches. A pitcher should examine it to see if it's tapered off sharper and gradually grades away to first and third base. If that makes a difference, the pitcher can get more power coming in off the rubber. Very close to the back end of the mound is the substance the pitcher is trying to dig into. The pitcher is constantly rooting it out and customizing it within the rules.

Players' bats have limited pine tar on them, I assume. Today bats don't splinter like they used to when Louisville Sluggers splintered badly. Today, umpires seem to scrutinize pitchers more often for foreign substances than in my day.

Once a player gets to the Big Leagues, he has probably developed relationships with many players, coaches, and umpires. The commissioners, players associations and the owners' meetings are giving players today more input into what they are doing. There is protection offered to a player who might be kept in the Minor Leagues for different reasons. It's not because they're the best position player or the best reliever or the best starting pitcher. It could be that they bring a certain dynamic. It keeps the team unified, and that keeps the players believing in one another.

Today there is more organization at the top because there is more money in the game. Paperwork was often lost in the shuffle in the 1960s but now with computers, there is no reason for data not to be available to managers, coaches, players, and player representatives. Movement between levels should be better organized, more informative, and more efficient than it was in the past. I would say movement between levels was slipshod when I played. Player stability was mostly uncertain.

Communications are essential and more convenient with email and cell phones. No excuses. A new pitcher coming in from the Minor Leagues would likely meet in the office with the manager and be provided with information of what is expected of him. He would know if he was a starter or reliever, and all the questions that he might have would be answered. He would know when he was going to start and how many days off he would have for rest. Scouts and player representatives would be involved in the conversations.

When I played, rookies and veterans were dealt with differently. If a player had never pitched in the Big Leagues before, there was an unwritten rule in some ballparks that rookies would be worked into the staff and perform certain responsibilities, such as batting practice, as they did in the Minor Leagues. If the pitching coach wasn't satisfied with how the rookie was performing, it could delay a starting opportunity. Rookies did not get a chance to pitch against first division ball clubs. There were ways to work a player into the lineup to see what he could do. There wasn't a rulebook on exactly what happened in a sequence. It was subjective. For example, if the team you were pitching against was a team that a pitcher should do well against, that didn't mean he would get to pitch. When he arrives at the ballpark, he must be ready to pitch.

Times change, the game evolves. Some of the changes are less obvious than others to the casual observer.

Those are my views.

69

SCOUTS

Scouts were very reputable when I played ball. They earned their living because of how they had played the game, or who they knew in the organizations around both leagues, including the Minor Leagues. They often had more insight into the ability of some of the players you heard about in the Minor Leagues. If the scout had a friend he played with, the friend might have an opportunity to scout, particularly if he was from the same hometown. It was preferable to have a scout who had a reputation of his own in his hometown. It would be terrible to have a player drafted or picked off from your town, and the scout not know anything about him. There were rumors about players who were released and had never been seen or promoted. If the scout did his homework and kept records, the statistics showed who should be looked at, moved up, or moved down.

An influential group was the press. If a local player was getting a lot of press, that would attract the attention of the scouts, and possibly scouts from different organizations would show up to watch and track the player. No press, no coverage, no chance for opportunity. My exceptional press coverage out of the Tri-County League catapulted me into the sights of two scouts. Unfortunately, the rest of my career had minimal press coverage even when I was performing at a high level.

With the expansion teams in the 1960s, more players were getting the opportunity to play. Players were coming from warm climates with many coming from South America. These players were talented and inexpensive, and therefore, popular with both scouts and owners.

Scouts were tight-lipped about what they saw, and rarely gave updates on players they were watching. They were always traveling, and we players didn't really know what they saw, or what they were looking for. Some scouts took the bus, some drove themselves, and others flew. We didn't know what kind of records and evaluations they had on individual players, and who they were sharing their observations with about the players.

It could be that the scouts were at a restaurant informally discussing players with colleagues, and those scouts might formulate an opinion based on another scout's analysis and observation of a player. Therefore, one could erroneously take an opinion and run with it to the detriment of the player. There wasn't a clear-cut plan for scouting that I was aware of: responsibilities, loyalties, recordkeeping, prejudices, serious analysis, and subjective opinion could all influence a player's progress. My speculation on the scouting process is that there was a lack of communication from the top down.

It wasn't until the late 1960s that Curt Flood, Marvin Miller, and Free Agency information, started to take hold of Major League baseball. Previously, Farm Directors had control of all players except high value bonus babies. Marvin Miller put Free Agency together along with the input from a few brave players. It took guts to put your beliefs on the line and not get deserved credit. I commend those guys for getting the job done. They were more adamant about being able to work their own deal and not have to cater to the team that bought and paid for them. When Kurt Flood became attractive to other clubs, he should have been able to work the deal, but that didn't happen.

My general impression as a player was that the Senators organization was kind of "catch as catch can." There was not a lot of consistency in management. Looking back it seemed like management was looking out for themselves and their next big move. The Senators organization was a stepping stone to something better. In contrast, the New York Yankees had consistent management and success. From 1945-1965, Del Webb, visionary businessman, baseball lover, and part owner of the New York Yankees, revitalized the Yankee organization, reforming baseball into a business with more structure and accountability. I've often thought that is why the Yankees won 10 World Series during the 20 years Webb was part owner.

Scouts did their part, but the organization could have been more productive and helpful, in my opinion.

70

OPTIONS

The organization of professional baseball in the 1960s has always baffled me: so many questions, so many unknowns. My understanding of how the system operated was limited, and felt concealed.

How the process worked from my perspective was that a player was evaluated and assigned to a particular league and level. That assignment was not necessarily binding depending on the evaluation. A player might be optioned to Winter Ball or Spring Training and then officially assigned to the league where management felt he could best perform. Details of his achievements at the league or college level might have influenced the decision.

Money may also have been a consideration. The organization would agree to pay X salary that included expense money for travel, meals, hotel, and family accommodations. If a player reached a higher level of proficiency, it might include playing in All-Star games, monthly incentives, and even promotion to a higher level. If a player reached a new level, there might be a bonus check given to entice him to sign a contract, and receive the total money agreed upon. Contracts were renegotiated every year that the player stayed with the organization. Any trades or agreements after the player signed the contract would revert back to the original agreement. That was my understanding.

The reserve clause in Major League Baseball had been in effect since the late 1800s and gave owners most of the options, and thus, control of players. They traded, sold, assigned or released players. Players could hold out or quit. Not many options.

The questions I had, and every player should have had are: who decides what happens to a player and what is the criteria for the decision? Why is the player not involved in decision-making that affects his entire career? Those questions were always on my mind, but never answered, or asked. There was a fear that asking questions or asking for accommodations could hinder a player's status. "Don't rock the boat" seemed to be a message I heard and understood. Today players have clarity about how their future is determined by management, thanks to Free Agency.

The intricacies of how management shifted players around was always bewildering. How was it determined that a player would move from one level to another based on his rating? A player might find out he is moving from Elmira to Watertown where the ratings are different. The player in the 1960s had little or no input into options from one classification to another. A player's position could be protected by elevating his status to Triple A level, Double A, or Single A. If he was attracting other organizations management would have to take him to the next level to protect him. These were owners' options. How the options were handled made a huge difference in one's travel through the organization: it could help advance, or hinder, progress.

Options

It would have been helpful to know how many options one had starting at the top. How many options or how many times the organization could option a player up and down the ladder was unknown to me. How many options a player might have at each level was a question players never got answered during the 1960s. For example, if a player started at class A level, how many times could the organization option him to a protected rating such as Triple A or Major League. Also, what information was included in that option for the other organizations to have to adhere to or be aware of? Was there any uniform criteria that was used by all players or was it merely subjective? If a situation occurred such as an injury or performance that was slightly elevated or reduced, how would that temporary change affect a players status? Often, if a player was moved up the ladder, it was because organizations were interested in him.

In looking back, it seems that this information would have been vital to consider prior to signing a contract. Understanding the commitment, family concerns, salaries, bonuses, and options were areas that needed to be addressed every year in the 1960s. I was on my own to navigate these areas most years. Bottom line for me was: take it or leave it.

71

PITCHING STAFF

One would expect managers to trade information on their pitchers and other players if they are being considered to move up or down. One would expect that they had meetings to decide who gets a chance to move up because not too many get that opportunity. One might expect that managers would tell each other something like this:

> How much has the pitcher pitched in the last week or two, and what was special about his improvement? There is documentation in writing that describes the successes. Is he comfortable with the new wind up? Has he worked on a few pick off moves in game situations to my satisfaction? One thing he needs now is 3 to 4 days rest. He has pitched eight out of nine days in games: spot start, long relief, short relief, and closer. Lastly, he has added a new pitch. That is part of the reason he

needs the extra rest. He is ready to go, in my opinion, back to the Big Leagues. No negatives. He just completed every task that we asked him to do. We should all have the same information. Any questions?

That's how I envisioned it should have happened.

But, it did not. It was a gross oversight by management and coaches. If it did happen, the player did not know about it, and the coaches and management did the usual, covered each other's asses. In the player's case, he didn't have the opportunity nor the flexibility to state any reason when asked about his pitching. It was obvious that a pitcher would not turn down an assignment given by the manager. The pitcher automatically assumed that the manager had made his decision based on information about his performance. Managers were often player position managers, who were not aware of the in-depth part of pitching. They knew the performance part but they didn't know the mental part that goes into it. Most of them were retired players.

As good as communications are today, I still don't think organizations and coaching staffs have a complete handle on some players. I do not think they have enough knowledge to make adjustments to pitchers who have different mechanical issues. Most players are built differently and very few throw the same way. You could watch John Drysdale throw and he looked like a slingshot. Jim Palmer, with the Orioles, was the same. The location from where the ball is released is delivered from the wind up. Leg conditioning, along with exercise conditioning, is essential.

Observation is critical. People who evaluate a player need to see that player from all angles: where he is standing, how he is pushing off the rubber. The rubber is the only point of contact with the ground. That is where he gets power, balance, and coordination.

Pitching Staff

Concentration is developed at certain times by pitchers in their careers. Some are blessed with it early. It's a natural thing for some of them, but mechanically might be a challenge for others. There are very few pitchers who do everything from the body they possess. The players who use their whole bodies stay around the longest. How they train, who they come in contact with, and what information is shared, or not shared, affects the pitcher's performance.

Rotation training needs to be known to staff and players. It should be matched according to players' abilities. Where do you back off training to get ready for your start? That can vary from pitcher to pitcher. There are players today, for example, who operate better on fewer days rest. They are the opposite of other pitchers who rely on extra days rest. It may be evaluated based on how hard they've trained. There should be observations to evaluate whether the pitcher is favoring one pitch or another. Maybe he needs an extra day's rest. An extra day's rest doesn't mean he doesn't do anything. It means he works the way he usually works. If the player was a reliever he has to get loose— about 70 pitches from the wind up and from the stretch. It's important to learn all the tasks: how fast a pitcher can get loose, and what is needed to make sure he's getting into the ballgame in relief.

The pitcher should have a baseball in his hand more than it's out of his hand, and that's a critical state. He has to maintain the feel of it. Some pitchers do it more than others. It's the grip, the way they throw the ball, and the side of the mound that they are on. All of these things contribute to his success or failure. It can be observed if it is watched very carefully when pitchers are warming up.

Mechanics are what baseball pitchers are all about. Pitchers with problems are the ones who are not mechanically solid. They are prone to injury because of the quirky way they do things. If they last long enough, exercise, train, eat properly, and get their rest, a lot of that can be rubbed out and built up. It depends on how much they've been involved earlier in the professional ranks, how much they accomplished, how many games they've been in, who the coaches are, and what's been written about them. Some clubs like awkwardness, but hitters do not. Those are the guys who drilled in on the deck circle or too close to home plate with a split-fingered fastball that slipped. Some pitchers are blessed with a lot of good talent from the start so the pitcher is not being tested in that regard. They need to throw side-armed, three-quarters, under the rubber, over the top, or whatever they need to do. Some athletes just have the ability and are effective. Location is something they have to prove to the coaches, umpires and managerial staff. If they've done that they make the ball club, or get traded.

A left-handed pitching coach should be added to the roster to work with left-handed pitchers. Most coaches are right-handed, but there are mechanics that affect left-handed pitchers differently. One pill does not work for most of your left-handed pitchers. Look in the mirror to see how it would look as a left-handed pitcher. How they perform is how you're going to be in or out of the ball game. If the pitcher is way ahead, just let him finish the game.

If your pitching staff needs rest, that's a different day off, but it can make a big difference in the entire staff. A one day rotation added to the pitching might be worthwhile. I've seen it work with the Washington Nationals early on when they brought someone up from Triple A because they had an extra game. They brought someone up at a certain time of the year. It may have been someone who was pitching well for them at Triple A but they don't have room on the 40 man roster. Maybe the lesser roster might be in place with 25 to 30, or maybe injured reserve would open up a spot. But it would be something extra. It's not changing up on your rotation. It's not asking a pitcher to step up and give you five or six innings because you have an extra game or you are traveling out west.

Learning how to bunt properly is important, and few players seem to be able to execute it these days. You do not stab at the ball. Line the bat up parallel to the ground and meet the ball. Push the ball forward into fair territory. It's like catching the ball. Bend the knees, lean toward the pitcher.

The pitching staff is vital to the success of the ball club, and no steps or stones should be left unturned until all the things I have suggested have been done. You do not have to be on the field to observe. You have to have one location where you can be placed and watch the players. A revolving camera that works may even be more helpful. The delivery, follow-through, time of observation, and balance need to be evaluated regularly by the organization's pitching gurus.

Keeping the left-handed pitching coach in the bullpen to observe what is going on with his players is going to pay dividends. Whatever they're paying pitching staffs today is never enough. After an injury, the club can basically farm you out. Good training and practices will keep that from happening.

The manager, owner, or whoever is going to sign the player, has to take chances. The difference between when I played and the present, is that today representatives take care of everything in negotiating a player's contract. In my day we had to be flexible and not get on the wrong side, because attitude was 70% of performance. If we had a good attitude and it stayed that way, it was positive. They would give you longer rope to get yourself in better condition. Some kiss ass cheats I did not have much contact with skated through. I would never have thought that was in the game, but that's how a few guys went about their trade.

    I was complete in my pitching, and 100% ready to have a second chance in 1967 to shove it up anybody's ass that needed it. I could control my pitches, start regularly, spot start, long relief, short relief, and close with proper rest between outings. What I could not do was pitch eight consecutive days and then start. A promise never kept, my career was burned at the stake.

72

THE SPONGE

If you are striving to become someone who has a reasonable future, this country offers that. It's there if you are willing to go after it. Think about always stepping forward, moving onto the next challenge.

Everyone is different with their attitudes, capabilities, and talents. We try to do what we think will help us, but there are limitations to what we can do entirely on our own. It's a learning process.

Anyone can be a mentor. Be receptive. I always thought of myself as a "sponge." I listened, absorbed, and tried any ideas that sounded reasonable to me. I got a late start in the game and worked hard to catch up. As a mentor, a small, positive comment can make a big difference in a young person's life.

Reaching goals may involve taking risks. Perhaps you have to move away from a small hometown for more options. Maybe you have to get involved in an organization because they offer training for something you want to do. There's no easy answer but it's important to take advantage of opportunities. You may not get a second chance.

No one is doing anything wrong. When I am talking to young players, I want to convey the thought that no matter what they are doing, if they are trying, they are not doing anything wrong. Perhaps they just need a boost in confidence, more training, more opportunities in order to improve. If they are encouraged, they build confidence. If there is confidence and a good attitude, success will follow. If you are improving, something is going right.

Your intestinal fortitude, your gratitude toward others, ability to forgive, receptiveness to advice, all should lead to successful results. In my life, people have offered opportunities, guidance, and encouragement. I also had to reach inside to motivate myself. No one is perfect. We do the best we can to accomplish our goals, and we should be satisfied that we gave it our best shot.

Positive thinking.

73

UMPIRES

When you enter a Major League ballpark or stadium you may notice the grounds crew and the field preparation that is occurring. If it is time for the game to begin the umpires show up but you probably don't recognize them as they look over the field prior to the start or even during batting practice. The umpire is examining the field to make sure it is in safe and proper condition. He must be aware of the weather and how it may affect the field. Are there areas that might be soft, waterlogged, or rough? Are the bases secured and the pitcher's mound safe and positioned correctly? The umpire is busy before the game even begins.

The umpire is the ultimate professional. He and his crew must maintain self-control at all times during the game, which is emotionally charged by its very nature; two talented teams geared up to take each other down! Plus, tens of thousands of fans are expecting great entertainment! The umpire has to manage both teams and the fans, not knowing what situations will arise that cause emotions to flare up. As the game evolves, the umpire has to listen to disputes and concerns, weigh the information, be aware of player safety, monitor changes in lineups, and calmly address the issues. If the umpire is uncertain about a call, he gets input from other umpires who may have had a better angle. Even with the use of instant replay technology, a decision may not be 100% correct.

Charlie Keller told me to never second-guess an umpire. Do not confront an umpire. Respect the decisions they make. They are human, but they are the ultimate decision maker for that game. Plus, if a player is confrontational, there is a good chance the umpire will remember. Most, if not all, of the umpires at the Major League level, are older and have been in the game for a long time. Chances are there is not much they haven't seen. All the more reason to not challenge their decisions.

There are times when a player, in the heat of the moment, makes a mistake or shows up an umpire. Gestures, curses, pushing, name-calling, and more, are serious offenses that a player should regret later. An umpire has a memory like an elephant, and, if you offended or challenged the umpire, he will remember. He will catch you when you need him the most.

When I came into the game as a 19 year old, I had an edge up on a lot of the rookies because I knew I was not going to challenge an umpire. If he missed a pitch or did not give me a call I thought I deserved, I was not going to do anything because he had a shot at me whenever he wanted to take it.

As a rookie, I had an awkward situation involving an umpire crew in our hotel bar. This particular umpire crew had worked my game earlier. One of the team veterans suggested I go over to the umpires' table, thank them for the great job they did in my game, buy them a drink, or share whatever feelings I had about the game they called.

I was thinking to myself, "Wait a minute. Is that what you do? Do you buy a round of drinks for the umpires? NO!"

I was a youngster, trying to figure that one out and it sounded like a bribe. I did not want them to think I was expecting them to do anything differently for my next game. It didn't make sense to me, and it was hard to justify. However, not knowing how the game was played from that perspective, I did go over and thank them for umpiring a well-controlled game. I believed that I should do my job and they should do their job and let the chips fall where they may. I was not about giving or taking bribes. Awkward.

Umpires and managers control the players. If the managers do not control the players, umpires will take care of that issue. Pitchers protect their own players. If the pitcher makes a good pitch and the batter hits it out, it hurts the entire club, even if it was a good pitch. It becomes a problem if the batter is celebrating or acting out because of his success. Everyone needs to be under control and give credit for a job well done.

Umpires are human and not always perfect but their decision for the day is the one that counts. There are times where an umpire will tell a catcher that he is having a bad day. He may be calling a tighter strike zone. But he does the best he can and that is the way it is.

A tricky situation for the pitcher is where an umpire limits the pitcher's options.

The umpire might tell a pitcher, "Hey, Lefty, No up and down. Just in and out."

The pitcher works harder because his arsenal of pitches is now limited. It happened to me so I personally knew how tough that outing was going to be. If you have a hitter who likes the ball low and the umpire is not calling strikes there, you are really in a squeeze. The average fan would not notice that limitation and might fault the pitcher.

It takes a mature, well-grounded, confident person to be an umpire, in my opinion. They have a lot to manage on game day and deserve everyone's total respect. Always.

74

APPRECIATION

There were people who gave my family and me comfort, help, and security when times were tough. Often, they had their own issues and hardships but they took the time to help us. We never truly knew where help might come from and the encouragement it gave us. I always felt that I wanted those who influenced me to be proud.

Life gets complicated. There's no question about that. Sometimes we make the complications ourselves. The decisions we make in a hurry may not be the wisest decisions we make, but he who hesitates is sometimes lost. When we are lost, we remember that loss and try to get back on the path to accomplish our goals. I also don't think we should beat ourselves up about a poor decision, if we can reverse it.

I think about the sacrifices that people make to help each other. I think about what people mean to others, and how important they are. Sometimes appreciation is not expressed nor recognized at the time because we don't know how beneficial the help was. It's unfortunate to recall the people who never were aknowledged for their contributions to you becoming who you are. People have come to our aid when we needed it and we are so thankful and humbled, but maybe we didn't acknowledge that soon enough.

If you take the time to tell people that you value what they did for you, and are sincere, it can be uplifting for both of you. I have reached out to people on my list and hope that there's a line of communication that continues after we leave this earth because what they did for me when they were here may have been hard to put into words at the time. Try to get it out. It's as simple as picking up the phone and calling those who have made a difference in your lifetime. I am 83. I know.

No excuses. No regrets. Do it today.

Part Four

PITCHING SPECIFICS AND MORE

Read the disclaimer at the beginning of the book.
Be smart. Be safe. Get a good instructor.
Know yourself. Stay healthy.

75

THINKING ABOUT PITCHING?

At nine years old there are few things that you have achieved to the point where your ability is greater than your confidence. Becoming a good pitcher, or "controller of the baseball," there may be tips that you have picked up by watching games in person or on TV. Announcers like Harry Carey, Bob Feller, and Jim Palmer describe the art of pitching a baseball effectively.

Certain body parts may develop faster than others. I am referring mainly to the strength that you may have developed in your arm, shoulders, back and legs, not to mention the vital function of your abdomen and lungs. This awareness may have to be taught. Of course, there are people who have natural ability, and their flexibility may put them in a better place than other young players. Hereditarily, there are physical make-ups that could help in areas of controlling the baseball. Ideas are planted in your mind as you talk to baseball fans, coaches, and players. Some of these folks have not achieved a lot in the game, but from observation and common sense, they may feel qualified to teach a young person how to pitch.

It's all about mechanics. I studied it by watching successful, veteran pitchers and experimenting until I mastered a skill. Today when I watch Major League baseball and see players struggling, it is usually related to mechanics. When I had a three-fingered glove and had to adapt it to suit my left hand, I was learning the importance of mechanics within my physical ability. There is not one perfect technique for every pitcher because of individual differences.

As you may recall, I did not want to pitch until I developed more control. Get a good instructor.

76

HOLD ON

*P*roper arm motion is essential in maximizing the baseball throwing motion.

First, you must hold the ball correctly. When you have small fingers, you may grab a ball with three fingers and a thumb, with the little fingers knuckled under the palm of your hand to rest the ball. Unless you have exceptionally long fingers, this is 90% of the way you begin to hold the baseball.

As you get older, you take those fingers off the baseball as soon as possible, leaving the middle and index fingers and thumb on the ball, with the first knuckle of the ring finger being used as a resting finger. If you have long fingers, this holding position may vary. What you have now is a position from which you can begin to take advantage of the seams on the baseball. In my opinion, here is where early success begins. Be careful to hold on because it will leave just as fast as you learned it. When I first joined the Army and didn't touch a baseball for several weeks, it took a while to get the feel of the baseball again.

The next step is crucial to moving forward and becoming a good thrower. Think of a javelin thrower or hitting a tennis ball overhead. You snap the wrist on the follow-through. Start by pointing your throwing arm towards second base. Picture yourself showing the bottom of your wrist and all the white that's on the baseball to second base. This position has the back of your hand facing you in as much of a right angle as you can create. The next move is to turn your hand over with your palm now facing up to the sky. Your wrist is also facing the sky and your arm is quickly under the baseball or javelin. You are in position to deliver the baseball.

The final position is as important as the others. You have to pull your hand forward along with your arm close to your ribs. Your hand is much like a slingshot. It is called "getting on top of the baseball," delivering it to home plate.

With these techniques, you will find that you will be high in the strike zone, if you are in it at all. Once you have this position, you will like the speed and it may be hard to stick it out, but now you know how to throw.

The next aspect to work on is to bring you down into the strike zone. It begins by having you throw into a pillow. Yes, your sleeping pillow— every night for 10 to 15 minutes, just snapping your wrist. Next, you should throw the ball to home plate, bending your back and almost touching the ground with your throwing hand. Throw at half speed or batting practice speed. Keep in mind, 12 pitches inside and 12 pitches to the outside corners of home plate. Stay between the hitter's belt and knees.

Next, do the same exercise from the stretch with men on base. In both positions, move your "push off" foot forward and back. Those inches may make the difference between a ball being fielded and a base hit. Baseball is a game of inches. Never forget that as long as you play. Rehearse, rehearse, rehearse with the supervision of a knowledgeable instructor.

77

HIDE IT

Pitchers must hide the baseball. You must be able to change the grip when the ball is hidden in your glove. Do not move the ball around for hitters or coaches to see. All the opposition needs to see is the back of your glove. You know what the grip should be for the pitch you want to throw.

Some pitchers set the ball in their glove and look over the glove with their pitching arm free. Justin Verlander is an example. Some use a "no wind up" and I was one of them. That is a pretty regular way to hide the baseball. It is hard to do when you already have the ball in your glove and then go into your glove, taking a stretch, or no wind up, and delivering the pitch.

Sometimes pitchers show the side of their wrist and opposing players pick up the sign by watching carefully from the dugout. The third base coach might pick up the white of the ball in your hand. Likewise, the first base coach might be able to see the ball so you have to make sure you hold the baseball the same way all the time. When you get the signal, you apply the grip automatically, just a simple rotation of the glove.

78

DELIVERY

I start with left-handed pitchers because I know what you need in almost every situation. Also, I want you to throw as few pitches as possible.

When the left-handed pitcher is mechanically sound, your body is rotating around your head, focused on home plate. Your shoulders are rotating with your hips, and the right knee is lifted toward the left hip. Step toward home plate. The right foot lands on the ball of the right foot, pointing directly to the spot where you are delivering the baseball. The right knee bends, lowering your entire frame or torso. Next, your the left leg comes out of the rubber and finishes even with the right foot. The objective is not letting the batter see the ball until the very last possible second. Arm action is next.

I like left-handed pitchers to stand back on the third base edge of the rubber to pitch against a right-handed hitter. At the same time I want you, my left-handed pitcher, to throw more overhand than 3/4 (side arm). If you are coming over the top with your arm by your ear, the ball is much easier to control, in my view. Also, the likelihood of movement from a left-hander is greater when you are up on top of the baseball with your arm coming into home plate. That is in a normal wind up (or no wind up) position that you would be in.

If you, the left-handed pitcher, throw from the left edge of the rubber, it brings the baseball in closer to the left-handed hitter. The weakness of learning to throw from the first base side of the rubber is that it opens up a better look for a right-handed batter to pick up the baseball. Normally, if you stay on the left edge of the rubber, addressing a right-handed batter, the pitcher wants to bring the ball hard to the batter's belt buckle. Let it run and there is a natural movement of the ball running back to the inside corner to a right-handed batter. That is not a good position to be in unless you are purposely trying to throw balls. The purpose should be to get the ball inside, but the chances of making a mistake are greater if you are on the third base edge of the rubber.

For a right-handed pitcher, you are going to be on the third base edge of the baseball pitching rubber. Then you can slide wherever you may be comfortable across the rubber, throwing from any angle, as long as you're in contact with the mound or rubber. In some cases you want to cut into the dirt that's in front of the mound against the rubber to give it the strength of your big toes. I say toes because that's the only contact you normally have. If you can keep the ball of your foot in that position, you'll be better at throwing because you'll spring out of the rubber. You will also be in position to field a baseball that may be hit back toward the mound or bunted down the first or third baselines.

When releasing the baseball, I wanted to get the ball out of my fingertips and pitch off the thumbnail. I did not want to pitch off the inner part of the thumb because my hand was adult-sized. The longer the thumb, the better chance the pitcher has of having the ball move with control and movement. Ideally, the thumb length should come above the palm or near the first joint of the palm. Since everyone is different, adjustments are made accordingly.

If something goes wrong, you should be able to fix it. A good pitching coach should be on top of you when your catcher signals by looking in the dugout. The catcher is in charge of communicating with the coach.

79

MOUND UP

*A*s a pitcher, I had to get the feel for the mound, the rubber, and the landing area. Figuring out where to stand on the rubber were skills to learn. I had to dig in the rubber without tearing it up, but still get a good push out of it. That's the only contact with the ground and where you get your power to home plate.

Adjusting to both sides of the rubber, and moving on the first base side of the rubber to a left-hander, and moving on the third base side of the rubber to a right-hander, was an adjustment that was difficult in my early professional baseball days. Using the middle rubber area for making slight adjustments, left or right or back-and-forth, was useful on days when I might be getting more movement on the ball or have flowing adrenaline. Knowing when and how to adjust was critical.

The pitcher's mound itself may vary in size, length, height, and may be movable and demand mechanical adjustments at some lower level ball parks. The mounds I played on were made out of dirt or clay, maybe mixed with some sand. Sometimes I had to adjust the mound before I played. Notice the mound. Be comfortable with it .

80

CONTROL YOURSELF

Controlling the baseball is as vital as common sense would dictate: awareness of your breathing, maintaining your grip, comfort with the mound and rubber, balance, throwing strikes, and so much more.

The main thing I worked on as a novice pitcher was control because I had problems with a smooth wind up. Be familiar with the mound. Only have your front spikes in the rubber area when you push off and pivot into your push off foot. This will work smoothly even with a hyperextended big toe. Believe me, I know! You don't have to have a gap between the rubber and the rubber mound, because then you lose power. Work on getting a follow-through position in your arm as close to your overhead as possible. That way, you are in better control.

You must land properly on your right leg in order to throw strikes as a left-handed pitcher. I had to overcome landing on my right heel as I threw the baseball because it immediately caused my head and body to bounce, and kept the ball from coming down and through the strike zone. I had to exaggerate pointing my right foot so I could land in the direction I was throwing the ball off my right foot and not on my right heel. Landing on my heel caused my head and body to bounce.

As a check, I asked myself: Was my chin on my chest? Had I rotated my body around my head?

I shouldn't jerk my head around and I was doing that without realizing it. I learned to rotate my body around my head. I had to make my wind up so that I reached for the target and followed through. The lower I followed through, the more effective the pitch was. I pointed my toe, landed on the ball of my right foot, and was ready to field the baseball in any direction. I always asked my catcher or another teammate to watch me as I checked off the list.

Once you come from the same spot with control, move around. Throw from the same spot until comfortable, eventually making the pitches from all spots.

Planning ahead is important. Understand what you are going to do and, if you have practiced effectively, you will do it.

81

STRIKE ZONE

What happens when you're constantly throwing in a spot and you're not getting strikes? You have to be flexible on the rubber. No matter what your achievement may be, there are days when your arm will be more alive. That doesn't mean you won't have good stuff. You can adapt and get good control. You just have to know what to do.

If you are constantly missing a spot, reposition yourself on the rubber. It doesn't have to be a lot. It just has to be enough to have you thinking you have corrected the problem. A good catcher will be there on the mound to tell you that advice: move over one way or the other, your arm is 3/4 when it should be straight over the top, you're dropping down slightly, below 3/4 somewhere in the area. That's going to give you a lot more movement but less control. You will give up some speed because you're cutting the ball as well. It may sink more or sail more but that depends on your rhythm, grip and the weather.

Major League Shutout Debut

Our goal is to throw strikes and we cannot stay out there very long if we can't throw strikes. There are a lot of left-handers who go through this struggle because they are left-handed and afraid of not being able to throw strikes. Why, you ask yourself? There will be no adjustment by the umpire. It's the movement of the baseball and the adjustment of your catcher. The catcher can't do a lot of movement when he has a hitter in the batter's box. He has to wait to the point of your wind up being halfway through, because the hitter should be in full concentration of where the baseball is coming from.

Some hitters keep a book on pitchers, and make sure they remember what you tried to do to get them out. As a pitcher, you should have a book on how you want to pitch to a certain hitter. Line up situations and create information about what hitters will try to do to drive a run in: Do they change? Are they looking for the ball in the spot and turning on it quickly? If they get it fair, great. If it goes foul, at least they got the swing and contact which is really working to their advantage. I look at it like it's to my advantage. I want them to pull the ball foul.

One of the biggest challenges you have is to get the ball out over the plate and avoid meeting the wood of the bat. No matter how the batter misses it, it will travel better with as much wood as he can get on it. It gives him a sacrifice fly, a tag up situation, or a homerun.

I've always believed the front corners of home plate are part of the strike zone. If the umpire bails out of his setup ahead of the pitch, he may miss a strike that catches the corner. Until the umpire recognizes the full strike zone, it's his call. As a pitcher, I'm always going to give umpires the respect they deserve, and not question the calls, ever.

82

ADVANCED AND GAME SITUATIONS

I am ahead in the count. If I've gone there with as hard stuff as I can, then I am apt to turn over a straight change up on the outside corner, depending on who the hitter is. It could also run and sink. If you have a power hitter, you're not going to want to give into that power. You're going to want to take that away with soft stuff, but show him the heat.

Smart hitters will watch from the on deck circle to see what the pitcher is throwing. Some hitters may wander out of the on deck circle to get a better look at the pitcher. I am okay with hitters as long as they stay in the circle. If the hitter moves out of the circle I may have to pull a "Bull Durham" with my ring finger. Getting an unfair advantage by getting behind the batter will not be tolerated.

Consequently, batters struggle when they get to the batter's box, or, moreover, they get behind the pitcher in the count. That is established by the pitcher which gives him a distinct advantage. If you are the pitcher, you want to be on top of the hitter. You are throwing strikes, getting ahead of the batter in the count.

The batter has to adjust and can't look for just one kind of pitch in a certain spot. He can only do that when he is ahead of you. As a pitcher, the hitter is going to look for the ball he can drive the best, and if he is not doing that, he hasn't learned the art of hitting. Looking for the baseball and having your body move for a hitter is a lot different. There are similarities to what your body has to do. With pitching for a nine inning game, you need: three innings with your legs, three innings with your breathing and rhythm, and three innings with your arm. Always concentrate.

In a situation with runners on first and second, with less than two outs, you want to be able to bunt the ball. That is what they call a "wheel rotation." The pitcher automatically moves toward third after throwing the ball home. He is fielding the ball. The third baseman fakes between the mound and back to third base. The pitcher normally fields the ball because that is where it's going. You can't let the third baseman have to field it unless it's bunted really hard. Then it's nobody's play. The pitcher just gets in the way. I don't remember screwing up any bunt situation throwing the ball away, except early when I was wild. It never happened once I learned how to field.

STAMINA is built in one of the innings pitched. There are times when you have to bear down a little harder than normal. You have to concentrate harder, but remain relaxed. You have to be flexible enough to rotate your body to maximize your coil delivery to the plate. These are rhythmic movements that must be developed.

The way to field the ball is with both hands. Don't reach with your glove. Fire that ball like you are throwing to home. That is something you have to learn. You have to be BALANCED and follow through. You may get in a rundown at first base. If there's nobody else on base, except first, you bounce out and get behind the first baseman as he's chasing down the runner. You have to stay behind the bag until he's out of the baseline. Then you jump in front, and you become the first baseman and work to get the guy out that you picked off. Know what the rules are for how many of your players can be in the baseline at one time. Pay attention.

83

ADVANCED–PICK OFF MOVES AND MORE

*W*hen you develop more pitches, you can vary the location of your fastball. You could still side arm your fastball if it is effective enough. If you had to sink, you could also throw a slider from that position. It may come up and in, which keeps the batter off the plate, and keeps the bat where he has no use for it. Move around after you become skilled at one spot. Learn your pick off moves early in your career, and practice them often with an experienced base runner.

Developing pick off moves, and a good move to home plate means BALANCE. You have to have BALANCE: be able to lift your front foot up as slow as possible, and then decide, if you haven't already, where you are going – to first base or home in a left-hander's position. A right-hander has to swivel his hips and rock backwards toward second base, and then come forward if someone is on second. The left-hander can do the same thing. He can roll back and the guy on first base gets a bigger lead. Your chances of getting a double play are reduced greatly if you try to swivel unless you are going to throw the ball or fake the ball to second.

You have to develop more than one move. A left-hander should have at least three pick off moves. That includes putting his hands together, going to the plate; putting his hands together, like he is going to first base, but looking home; and putting his hands together, looking at home hard, and then going to first base. BALANCE is the key to success. Lifting the front leg slowly freezes the runner so he can't go. You need a first base coach with a big mouth so he can yell "Get back!" if the runner goes. BALANCING through the middle allows you to defend yourself and also make plays. It allows you to get off the mound.

You don't have to throw to any base but home or first. When you throw towards home, the ball must continue towards home. If you hold onto it, it will be a balk. Sometimes guys lose balance, ball or grip. Tough day.

Another focus is what I call pitching uphill. Your stomach keeps you from bending toward home plate. Overcome that by keeping your chin on your chest and leaning into the pitch rather than backing off and coming through from second base. It makes you more effective and lets your body work better. Those pitchers who are 6'8" to 6'10" don't have to worry, like Cubs player, Ferguson Jenkins. Jim Kaat, Twins pitcher, was big on the mound as well. He had a bowlegged delivery and a tap dancer motion. He consistently threw strikes, and did very well.

You are more in control of the game when you have good balance and movement.

84

FINAL THOUGHTS

Almost every day I have a recollection from my days of playing baseball. Here are some of my latest "final" thoughts.

Nothing is simple in the game of baseball. Many people say it's a boring game. For them, it may be relaxing to watch the game and not focus on the ongoing strategic maneuvers. Positioning is happening with every pitch. Outfielders are shifting into positions where they anticipate the ball is going to end up. How many times have you seen a player standing still when a ball is fouled off? They should have at least flinched in a direction because there is a lot to do when contact is made with the baseball by the hitter. Observe.

100% is what I wanted to be and tried to be every time I went out to pitch. I expected that I could win. There were days in which no matter how hard I tried it just wasn't my day. If you can get 80% to 90% with all your pitches, good luck. Throwing toward 90 mph with great training is a good goal. I believe any difficulties are correctable. Good instruction should be beneficial.

Finally!

Go with your best stuff. You never want someone to beat you with anything but your best stuff!

85

DON LOUN PITCHING STATS (1961-69)

Year	W-L	ERA	G	GS	CG	IP	H	R	HR	BB	SO	SHO	Class Team
1961	5 - 3	5.33	1	14	1	81	67	53	5	75	63	1	D Pensacola Senators
1962	11 - 9	3.67	23	23	7	162	118	102	9	126	177	1	A Pensacola Senators
1963	11 - 10	3.32	32	29	8	178	161	91	10	107	143	5	A Peninsula
1964	Y: 6 - 5 T: 4 - 3	Y: 2.54 T: 1.47	Y: 14 T: 11	Y: 14 T: 8	Y: 5 T: 1	Y: 92 T: 55	Y: 79 T: 47	Y: 31 T: 19	Y: 2 T: 4	Y: 50 T: 17	Y: 79 T: 32	Y: 2 T: 0	York AA Toronto AAA
1964	1-1	.500	2	2	1	13	13	4	0	3	3	1	Major League Washington Senators
1965	6 - 12	4.46	26	21	5	127	123	72	12	72	57	0	Hawaii AAA
1966	H: 2 - 2 Y: 4 - 7	H: 9.00 Y: 6.03	H: 6 Y: 28	H: 6 Y: 14	H: 0 Y: 3	H: 23 Y: 94	H: 30 Y: 101	H: 25 Y: 76	H: 4 Y: 9	H: 18 Y: 71	H: 12 Y: 66	H: 0 Y: 0	Hawaii AAA York AA
1967	Y: 3 - 7 H: 0 - 0	Y: 2.49 H: 3.00	Y: 22 H: 2	Y: 6 H: 2	Y: 4 H: 0	Y: 76 H: 9	Y: 69 H: 7	Y: 29 H: 3	Y: 1 H: 1	Y: 24 H: 3	Y: 63 H: 7	Y: 0 H: 0	York AA Hawaii AAA
1968	0 - 3	5.43	21	5	0	53	57	45	9	32	37	0	Buffalo AAA
1969	0 - 1	4.50	11	0	0	22	15	15	1	0	17	0	Savannah AA

Credit: baseball-reference.com

EPILOGUE

"Lefty, you've been released." The abrupt end of one chapter of my life and the beginning of another. At age 28, it was time to move on. My professional baseball career was over. When I got home to Frederick, I began working the next day at Bechtel Corporation as a grader, a job I had held in the off-season. My new focus was to work hard and make a living. Baseball was on the back burner.

Soon I began a 36 year career in sales and management in the brick and block industry, beginning at MJ Grove Lime Company in Frederick (the future Genstar Corporation), where I interviewed to be a sales representative. In the spring of 1970, I met the love of my life, Kathleen. We raised a daughter and have been married for over 50 years. Over the years I have volunteered as a pitching instructor at local high schools.

Major League Shutout Debut

One of my favorite pictures of my daughter, Elizabeth, and me

As one of the twelve founding members of the Major League Baseball Players Alumni Association, I am proud of the growth and altruistic contributions the organization has made to baseball. According to their website, the nonprofit's mission is to "promote the game of baseball, raise money for charity, inspire and educate youth through positive sports images, and protect the dignity of the game through former players." I am pleased to have been able to organize and run a few golf tournaments during the early years of the organization.

Epilogue

Credit: https://www.mlb.com/mlbpaa/about/mission#

The Crackerjack Old Timer's Classic baseball game at RFK Stadium in 1982 brought back former players and memories of baseball days in Washington, DC. The most memorable moment had to be when 75-year-old, Hall of Famer, Luke Appling, hit a home run. He said afterwards that hitting that home run was one of the highlights of his life!

I am proud to be a lifetime member of the Association of Professional Ball Players of America organization. It is a nonprofit organization that focuses on ball players helping each other. It includes ball players from both the Major and Minor Leagues.

In 1999, I was proud to have been inducted into the Alvin G. Quinn Sports of Fame in Frederick. My values, ethics, and many of my opportunities are a result of the guidance of fine people in Frederick County who saw promise in me.

Major League Shutout Debut

Baseball became a new focus of mine in 2005 with the return of the sport to the DC area. The Washington Nationals played their first three seasons at RFK Stadium, which was the home of the Senators from 1962 to 1971. RFK Stadium was where I had my memorable debut in 1964. Coincidentally, exactly forty-three years later to the day I had pitched my shutout debut, there was a farewell celebration before the Washington Nationals played their last game at RFK. Former Washington Senators players, including myself, were invited to join the current Washington Nationals players on the field. Home plate was dug out and sent to the new stadium, Nationals Park. My family and I enjoyed the day of celebration with former teammates and local dignitaries. Over 50,000 fans were in attendance on a very special day that culminated with a colorful fireworks display.

My family with Washington DC mayor Anthony Williams at RFK Stadium, 2005

Epilogue

Over the years I have had opportunities to interact with former players, often while playing in charity golf tournaments. The annual Cal Ripken Sr. Foundation gala has been a great way to support the foundation's mission to help at-risk youth. The Baltimore Orioles Alumni Association meetings have provided nostalgic opportunities to keep in touch with players from my era. More recently, particularly as I have been writing, I have renewed memories with former teammates through phone calls and messages.

Recently, I learned that I am one of 250 athletes from Frederick County, MD who will be depicted on the Frederick Sports Mural, a huge painting on the outside perimeter of the Nymeo Field at Harry Grove Stadium featuring distinguished Frederick County athletes and coaches from the past 125 years. The mural project is a work in progress with supporting donations welcomed.

Watching and attending the Washington Nationals' games has been nostalgic. My family enjoys my frequent color commentary; there's so much to observe happening on and off the field!

My family at Nationals Park, 2019

Major League Shutout Debut

I have always believed that things turn out for the best. Although my baseball career did not fulfill my dreams as I had hoped, I have had a great life, far better than I ever imagined while daydreaming in the timothy fields years ago.

MOSTLY FAMILIAR NAMES

Some names are familiar locally and some names are known more universally. But all of them are people who I enjoyed playing baseball with or met along the way. They are remembered by me and many others.

Sam Moore was an attorney I met in the early 1970s. Sam's love of baseball and his impressive qualifications made him an ideal match for the newly-formed MLBPAA, the Major League Baseball Players Alumni Association, formed in 1982. Co-founders and former Washington Senators, Chuck Hinton and Jim Hannan, agreed, and Sam remained became our legal counsel for over 40 years. As one of the twelve founding MLBPAA members, I was pleased to have recommended Sam.

Major League Shutout Debut

Sam Moore, MLBPAA attorney
Credit: *Major League Baseball Players Alumni Association*

Jim Kaat, former pitcher for the Minnesota Twins and National Baseball Hall of Fame member, was a president of the MLBPAA. He was a fair, low key, regular guy. After baseball, Jim had become one of the best, impartial, radio announcers I had ever heard. Jim reminded me, "Once a Major Leaguer, always a Major Leaguer." Not every professional baseball player is a familiar name!

National Baseball Hall of Fame third baseman Brooks Robinson, a friendly, competent man, was also a longtime former president of the MLBPAA. On one occasion Brooks and I met with "Vinegar Bend" Mizell, former left-handed pitcher and Executive Director of President Reagan's Council on Physical Fitness and Sports. Brooks and I had invited Mizell to become a member of MLBPAA. While at his office I told Vinegar Bend that, as a kid, I always thought his name was odd and that he must be in the still business, making moonshine. Two very talented, down-to-earth athletes.

At a MLBPAA sponsored charity golf tournament, Mickey Mantle was the featured celebrity with whom each foursome played a par three hole. Mickey hit his shot 12 feet from the hole, the best of our group! An enjoyable outing with a baseball legend and skillful golfer.

Frank Howard, the true "gentle giant." He was an amazing player with a great sense of humor. I loved it when Shirley Povich, Washington Post sports reporter, interviewed "Hondo" about his workout routine and he answered Povich saying he put five pound weights in his shoes when he ran sprints!

Jim French. When I had my best outings, he was my catcher. He had all the tools for a long career in the Majors.

Eddie Brinkman and John Kennedy were a pair of teammates who could have been called Pete and Repeat. I can still picture them together smoking their new wood-tipped Hav-A-Tampa "Tampa Jewel" cigars.

Billy Hunter, from Baltimore, was the first professional baseball coach I worked with. I met him just before I signed a professional contract with the Washington Senators.

Bobby Richardson, New York Yankees second baseman. When I was an amateur, I thought Bobby projected an image I expected of all baseball players. He was polite, clean cut, and professional. The real deal.

Howie Bedell, Minor League coach for the York White Roses, taught me how to run on my toes and effectively steal bases. He was technically one of the best base runners I ever knew.

The Keller family of Frederick, Maryland, had many family members who crossed paths with me during my baseball years, including Charlie Keller ll, Hal Keller, and classmates, Charlie Keller lll and Donnie Keller.

Special thanks to Bryan Hissey for his efforts to put my name forward for the Alvin G. Quinn Sports Hall of Fame in Frederick.

There are many guys who were part of my Frederick sports history: Rudell Ahalt, John Carpenter, Gene Geisler, Ronnie Hart, Bill Krone, Harv McCutcheon, Tinker Michaels, Donnie Neal, Russell Rice, Chiz Staley and Paul Stroup. If you don't see a name, it may be in the early pages of my book. I apologize if I left out a few. So many special guys.

Familiar professional players who influenced me on or off the field included: Bernie Allen, Paul Blair, Tim Cullen, Willie Kirkland, Bobby Klaus, Bob Lipski, Walt Masterson, Bill Mazeroski, Jerry McNertney, Cal Ripken, Bobby Schantz, and Del Unser.

Tomorrow is another day. I'm sure I will recall another familiar name.

ACKNOWLEDGMENTS

Special people who inspired and supported my writing include the following:

Kathleen, my patient, thoughtful, selfless, and truly beautiful wife. Thank you for pushing me through to finish the story I started so many years ago. I couldn't have done it without you.

Elizabeth, my talented daughter, and biggest fan. Thanks for loving baseball and listening to my stories.

Corey, my clever son-in-law. Thank you for being a creative problem-solver who always surprises me.

Rob and Rick, my loyal nephews. I hope this book makes you proud.

Carlos, "The Chief" Medrano, my friend, roommate, teammate, and Best Man. Thank you for reminding me of the memories I forgot, listening to the ones I remember that you forgot, and enjoying the ones we both remember.

Bill Seidling, friend and former professional baseball catcher. Thank you for remembering and sharing information about our hometown of Frederick, Maryland.

Douglas Williams, friend and author of numerous baseball books. Thanks for listening and encouraging me to write my own story.

Alden Starnes, Associate Professor of Mathematics at Carson-Newman University. Thanks for perusing my career statistics and asking, "What happened?" in disbelief. It woke me up.

James R. Hartley, author of *Washington's Expansion Senators, (1961-1971)*. Thanks for the "how to" writing outline you gave me years ago.

Dave Fudge, David Fudge Photography. Thank you for your creative photography and your friendship.

Ray Plate, artist. Thank you for the amazing portrait you created.

Billy Staples, educator and baseball writer. Thank you for your dedication to promoting baseball for all ages.

Art Blum, author. Thanks for assuring me it was OK to tell my story "my way," as you do in your books.

Geoff Hixson, COO, Major League Baseball Players Alumni Association. Thanks for helping the ball players keep in touch with one another.

Sue Brewer, Artist. Thank you for creating drawings that I could only imagine.

Joe Rodriguez, coach, teacher and avid reader. Thanks for your thoughtful comments and questions after reading my manuscript.

Derek Gee, librarian, Maryland Room, C. Burr Arts Library, Frederick, Maryland. Thanks for uncovering news articles from my early years.

Joshua R. Smith, Sports Editor, Frederick News-Post newspaper. Thanks for your support in locating information for my book.

Made in the USA
Columbia, SC
05 January 2025

9856910e-cb3d-4df5-b33b-7f6ca5ea7590R01